LIGHT FOR
MY PATH

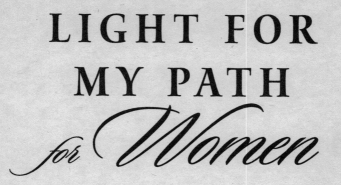

for Women

Illuminating Selections from the Bible

P9-DDB-109

HUMBLECREEK
INSPIRATION FOR LIFE

Compiled by Jennifer Hahn

© 2002 by Barbour Publishing, Inc.

ISBN 1-58660-643-3

Cover image © PhotoDisc.

Previously published as *The Bible Promise Book for Women*.

Unless otherwise noted, Scripture quotations are taken from the King James Version of the Bible.

Published by Humble Creek, P.O. Box 719, Uhrichsville, Ohio 44683

Printed in the United States of America.
5 4 3 2 1

Contents

Introduction

Our world sends many conflicting signals on the important issues of life. How should we approach anger? Is discipline a good thing or not? Why speak with honesty? Is prayer for real? What is true wisdom?

In His kindness, God has answered all of these questions—and many more—in the pages of His Word, the Bible. Whatever our needs, we can find in Scripture the principles we need to address the issues we face.

This collection of Bible verses is a handy reference to some of the key issues that all people—and especially women—face. In these pages, you'll find carefully selected verses that address topics like comfort, encouragement, friendship, purity, rest, and understanding. In fact, more than five dozen categories are covered, arranged alphabetically for ease of use.

This book is not intended to replace regular, personal Bible study. Nor is it a replacement for a good concordance for in-depth study of a particular subject. It is, however, a quick reference to some of the key issues of life that women most often face. We hope it will be an encouragement to you as you read.

All Scripture is taken from the King James Version of the Bible.

Adversity

Our Creator never intended that
we should shoulder a load of suffering ourselves.
That's the whole purpose of spiritual community.

LINDA BARTLETT

For I reckon that the sufferings of this present time are not worthy to be compared with the glory which shall be revealed in
us.   ROMANS 8:18

For as the sufferings of Christ abound in us, so our consolation
also aboundeth by Christ.

   And whether we be afflicted, it is for your consolation and
salvation, which is effectual in the enduring of the same sufferings which we also suffer: or whether we be comforted, it is for
your consolation and salvation.   2 CORINTHIANS 1:5–6

The righteous cry,
and the Lord heareth,
and delivereth them out of all their troubles.

PSALM 34:17

These things I have spoken unto you, that in me ye might have
peace. In the world ye shall have tribulation: but be of good
cheer; I have overcome the world.   JOHN 16:33

But the God of all grace, who hath called us unto his eternal
glory by Christ Jesus, after that ye have suffered a while, make
you perfect, stablish, strengthen, settle you.   1 PETER 5:10

Is any among you afflicted? let him pray.   JAMES 5:13

If ye be reproached for the name of Christ, happy are ye; for the spirit of glory and of God resteth upon you: on their part he is evil spoken of, but on your part he is glorified.   1 PETER 4:14

But what things were gain to me, those I counted loss for Christ.
    Yea doubtless, and I count all things but loss for the excellency of the knowledge of Christ Jesus my Lord: for whom I have suffered the loss of all things, and do count them but dung, that I may win Christ,
    And be found in him. . . .
    That I may know him, and the power of his resurrection, and the fellowship of his sufferings, being made conformable unto his death;
    If by any means I might attain unto the resurrection of the dead.   PHILIPPIANS 3:7–11

Blessed are ye, when men shall hate you, and when they shall separate you from their company, and shall reproach you, and cast out your name as evil, for the Son of man's sake.   LUKE 6:22

For our light affliction, which is but for a moment, worketh for us a far more exceeding and eternal weight of glory.
                                                    2 CORINTHIANS 4:17

Yea, and all that will live godly in Christ Jesus shall suffer persecution.   2 TIMOTHY 3:12

That the trial of your faith, being much more precious than of gold that perisheth, though it be tried with fire, might be found unto praise and honour and glory at the appearing of Jesus Christ.   1 PETER 1:7

Beloved, think it not strange concerning the fiery trial which is to try you, as though some strange thing happened unto you:

But rejoice, inasmuch as ye are partakers of Christ's sufferings; that, when his glory shall be revealed, ye may be glad also with exceeding joy.   1 PETER 4:12–13

For this is thankworthy, if a man for conscience toward God endure grief, suffering wrongfully. . . .

For even hereunto were ye called: because Christ also suffered for us, leaving us an example, that ye should follow his steps:

Who did no sin, neither was guile found in his mouth:

Who, when he was reviled, reviled not again; when he suffered, he threatened not; but committed himself to him that judgeth righteously.   1 PETER 2:19, 21–23

If we suffer, we shall also reign with him.   2 TIMOTHY 2:12

Heavenly Father,

I feel the darkness encompassing me.
The burden is so heavy to bear.
I thank You that You have promised to
take this weight from me.
I will surrender it to You,
leaving it in Your loving hands.
Amen.

Angels

On life's busy thoroughfares
We meet with angels
unawares. . . .

HELEN STEINER RICE

But to which of the angels said he at any time, Sit on my right hand, until I make thine enemies thy footstool?

Are they not all ministering spirits, sent forth to minister for them who shall be heirs of salvation?

HEBREWS 1:13–14

For I am persuaded, that neither death, nor life, nor angels, nor principalities, nor powers, nor things present, nor things to come,

Nor height, nor depth, nor any other creature, shall be able to separate us from the love of God, which is in Christ Jesus our Lord.   ROMANS 8:38–39

For he shall give his angels charge over thee, to keep thee in all thy ways.   PSALM 91:11

Let no man beguile you of your reward in a voluntary humility and worshipping of angels, intruding into those things which he hath not seen, vainly puffed up by his fleshly mind.

COLOSSIANS 2:18

Lord,

Thank You for Your protection.
I feel so valued when I consider that You
have appointed angels to guard me
and keep me safe.
Amen.

Anger

Being angry or unforgiving makes it impossible
to have a gentle and quiet spirit.

DARLENE WILKINSON

He that is slow to wrath is of great understanding: but he that is hasty of spirit exalteth folly.　　　　PROVERBS 14:29

Wherefore, my beloved brethren, let every man be swift to hear, slow to speak, slow to wrath:
　For the wrath of man worketh not the righteousness of God
.　　　　JAMES 1:19–20

Make no friendship with an angry man; and with a furious man thou shalt not go:
　Lest thou learn his ways, and get a snare to thy soul.
　　　　PROVERBS 22:24–25

B e not hasty in thy spirit to be angry:
for anger resteth in the bosom of fools.

ECCLESIASTES 7:9

It is better to dwell in the wilderness, than with a contentious and an angry woman.　　　　PROVERBS 21:19

Fathers, provoke not your children to anger, lest they be discouraged.　　　　COLOSSIANS 3:21

A soft answer turneth away wrath: but grievous words stir up anger.　　　　PROVERBS 15:1

Do all things without murmurings and disputings.

PHILIPPIANS 2:14

A wrathful man stirreth up strife: but he that is slow to anger appeaseth strife.

PROVERBS 15:18

But I say unto you, That whosoever is angry with his brother without a cause shall be in danger of the judgment: and whosoever shall say to his brother, Raca, shall be in danger of the council: but whosoever shall say, Thou fool, shall be in danger of hell fire.

MATTHEW 5:22

He that is slow to anger is better than the mighty; and he that ruleth his spirit than he that taketh a city.

PROVERBS 16:32

Dearly beloved, avenge not yourselves, but rather give place unto wrath: for it is written, Vengeance is mine; I will repay, saith the Lord.

ROMANS 12:19

Better is a dry morsel, and quietness therewith, than an house full of sacrifices with strife.

PROVERBS 17:1

Be ye angry, and sin not: let not the sun go down upon your wrath.

EPHESIANS 4:26

Father,

I didn't keep my anger in check.
I'm sorry that I failed You.
Please help me to guard my tongue
so that I don't used harsh words
to inflict pain on others.
Amen.

Charity

Charity begins at home.

PROVERB

Blessed is he that considereth the poor: the LORD will deliver him in time of trouble.

The LORD will preserve him, and keep him alive; and he shall be blessed upon the earth: and thou wilt not deliver him unto the will of his enemies.   PSALM 41:1–2

He that hath pity upon the poor
lendeth unto the Lord;
and that which he hath given
will he pay him again.

PROVERBS 19:17

But when thou makest a feast, call the poor, the maimed, the lame, the blind:

And thou shalt be blessed; for they cannot recompense thee: for thou shalt be recompensed at the resurrection of the just.   LUKE 14:13–14

He that despiseth his neighbour sinneth: but he that hath mercy on the poor, happy is he.   PROVERBS 14:21

I have shewed you all things, how that so labouring ye ought to support the weak, and to remember the words of the Lord Jesus, how he said, It is more blessed to give than to receive.
                    ACTS 20:35

He hath dispersed, he hath given to the poor; his righteousness endureth for ever. PSALM 112:9

I have been young, and now am old; yet have I not seen the righteous forsaken, nor his seed begging bread.
He is ever merciful, and lendeth; and his seed is blessed.
PSALM 37:25–26

Charge them that are rich in this world, that they be not high-minded, nor trust in uncertain riches, but in the living God, who giveth us richly all things to enjoy;
That they do good, that they be rich in good works, ready to distribute, willing to communicate;
Laying up in store for themselves a good foundation against the time to come, that they may lay hold on eternal life.
1 TIMOTHY 6:17–19

Sell that ye have, and give alms; provide yourselves bags which wax not old, a treasure in the heavens that faileth not, where no thief approacheth, neither moth corrupteth.
For where your treasure is, there will your heart be also.
LUKE 12:33–34

Above all things have fervent charity among yourselves: for charity shall cover the multitude of sins.
Use hospitality one to another without grudging.
As every man hath received the gift, even so minister the same one to another, as good stewards of the manifold grace of God.
1 PETER 4:8–10

Give, and it shall be given unto you; good measure, pressed down, and shaken together, and running over, shall men give into your bosom. For with the same measure that ye mete withal it shall be measured to you again.   LUKE 6:38

Thank You, Lord,
for all of the blessings You have given to me.
You have made me responsible for these blessings,
but they ultimately belong to You.
Help me to share them with others.
Amen.

Comfort

All you really need is
the One who promised
never to leave or forsake you—
the One who said,
"Lo, I am with you always."

JONI EARECKSON TADA

Yea, though I walk through the valley of the shadow of death, I will fear no evil: for thou art with me; thy rod and thy staff they comfort me.   PSALM 23:4

And God shall wipe away all tears from their eyes; and there shall be no more death, neither sorrow, nor crying, neither shall there be any more pain: for the former things are passed away.
                                                    REVELATION 21:4

The Lord GOD will wipe away tears from off all faces.
                                                    ISAIAH 25:8

For the Lord himself shall descend from heaven with a shout, with the voice of the archangel, and with the trump of God: and the dead in Christ shall rise first:
    Then we which are alive and remain shall be caught up together with them in the clouds, to meet the Lord in the air: and so shall we ever be with the Lord.
    Wherefore comfort one another with these words.
                                        1 THESSALONIANS 4:16–18

Casting all your care upon him; for he careth for you.
                                                    1 PETER 5:7

Comfort ye, comfort ye my people, saith your God.
                                                    ISAIAH 40:1

In the multitude of my thoughts within me thy comforts delight my soul.   PSALM 94:19

Blessed are they that mourn: for they shall be comforted.
                                                    MATTHEW 5:4

And I will pray the Father, and he shall give you another Comforter, that he may abide with you for ever.   JOHN 14:16

I would seek unto God, and unto God would I commit my cause.   JOB 5:8

Thou shalt increase my greatness, and comfort me on every side.   PSALM 71:21

The Spirit of the Lord GOD is upon me; because the LORD hath anointed me to preach good tidings unto the meek; he hath sent me to bind up the brokenhearted, to proclaim liberty to the captives, and the opening of the prison to them that are bound;

To proclaim the acceptable year of the LORD, and the day of vengeance of our God; to comfort all that mourn.
                                                       ISAIAH 61:1–2

And, lo, I am with you alway, even unto the end of the world.
                                                       MATTHEW 28:20

I will not leave you comfortless: I will come to you.
                                                       JOHN 14:18

Come unto me, all ye that labour and are heavy laden, and I will give you rest.   MATTHEW 11:28

I remembered thy judgments of old, O LORD; and have comforted myself.   PSALM 119:52

As one whom his mother comforteth, so will I comfort you.
                                                       ISAIAH 66:13

Blessed be God, even the Father of our Lord Jesus Christ, the Father of mercies, and the God of all comfort;

Who comforteth us in all our tribulation, that we may be able to comfort them which are in any trouble, by the comfort wherewith we ourselves are comforted of God.

For as the sufferings of Christ abound in us, so our consolation also aboundeth by Christ.   2 CORINTHIANS 1:3–5

Be perfect, be of good comfort, be of one mind, live in peace; and the God of love and peace shall be with you.

2 CORINTHIANS 13:11

Draw nigh to God, and he will draw nigh to you.

JAMES 4:8

Dear God,
*thank You for sending Your Comforter to soothe my hurting.
I don't need to look to earthly friends for help, although
You have given those who support me in the worst of times.
You are always just a prayer away, and
even when I can't think of the right words,
You still understand me.
Thank You, Lord.
Amen.*

CONVERSATION

K ind words can be short
and easy to speak,
but their echoes are
truly endless.

MOTHER TERESA

Even so the tongue is a little member, and boasteth great things. Behold, how great a matter a little fire kindleth!

JAMES 3:5

A word fitly spoken is like apples of gold in pictures of silver.

PROVERBS 25:11

Be not rash with thy mouth, and let not thine heart be hasty to utter any thing before God: for God is in heaven, and thou upon earth: therefore let thy words be few.

ECCLESIASTES 5:2

Let your speech be alway with grace,
seasoned with salt,
that ye may know how ye ought to
answer every man.

COLOSSIANS 4:6

A soft answer turneth away wrath: but grievous words stir up anger.   PROVERBS 15:1

The heart of the wise teacheth his mouth, and addeth learning to his lips.

Pleasant words are as an honeycomb, sweet to the soul, and health to the bones.   PROVERBS 16:23–24

The heart of the righteous studieth to answer: but the mouth of the wicked poureth out evil things.   PROVERBS 15:28

For he that will love life, and see good days, let him refrain his tongue from evil, and his lips that they speak no guile.
                                                        1 PETER 3:10

Let your conversation be without covetousness; and be content with such things as ye have.   HEBREWS 13:5

A talebearer revealeth secrets: but he that is of a faithful spirit concealeth the matter.   PROVERBS 11:13

In the multitude of words there wanteth not sin: but he that refraineth his lips is wise.   PROVERBS 10:19

A fool uttereth all his mind: but a wise man keepeth it in till afterwards.   PROVERBS 29:11

But now ye also put off all these; anger, wrath, malice, blasphemy, filthy communication out of your mouth.
                                                        COLOSSIANS 3:8

Set a watch, O LORD, before my mouth; keep the door of my lips.   PSALM 141:3

There is that speaketh like the piercings of a sword: but the tongue of the wise is health.   PROVERBS 12:18

If any man offend not in word, the same is a perfect man, and able also to bridle the whole body.   JAMES 3:2

For though I would desire to glory, I shall not be a fool; for I will say the truth: but now I forbear, lest any man should think of me above that which he seeth me to be, or that he heareth of me.   2 CORINTHIANS 12:6

A man hath joy by the answer of his mouth: and a word spoken in due season, how good is it!   PROVERBS 15:23

A time to rend, and a time to sew; a time to keep silence, and a time to speak.   ECCLESIASTES 3:7

Lord,
help me to control my speech.
I need Your help in remembering that
even the smallest word can cause great pain.
Guard my tongue,
so that I may be a woman of God who is
known as an encourager to others.
Amen.

Counsel

The true secret
of giving advice is,
after you have honestly
given it, to be perfectly
indifferent whether it is taken or not,
and never persist
in trying to set people right.

HANNAH WHITALL SMITH

As every man hath received the gift, even so minister the same one to another, as good stewards of the manifold grace of God.
1 PETER 4:10

For unto us a child is born, unto us a son is given: and the government shall be upon his shoulder: and his name shall be called Wonderful, Counsellor, The mighty God, The everlasting Father, The Prince of Peace.   ISAIAH 9:6

Where no counsel is,
the people fall:
but in the multitude of
counsellors there is safety.

PROVERBS 11:14

And all thy children shall be taught of the LORD; and great shall be the peace of thy children.   ISAIAH 54:13

Now no chastening for the present seemeth to be joyous, but grievous: nevertheless afterward it yieldeth the peaceable fruit of righteousness unto them which are exercised thereby.
HEBREWS 12:11

Hear counsel, and receive instruction, that thou mayest be wise in thy latter end.   PROVERBS 19:20

Howbeit when he, the Spirit of truth, is come, he will guide you into all truth: for he shall not speak of himself; but whatsoever he shall hear, that shall he speak: and he will shew you things to come.   JOHN 16:13

Give instruction to a wise man, and he will be yet wiser: teach a just man, and he will increase in learning.   PROVERBS 9:9

Brethren, if a man be overtaken in a fault, ye which are spiritual, restore such an one in the spirit of meekness; considering thyself, lest thou also be tempted.   GALATIANS 6:1

The way of a fool is right in his own eyes: but he that hearkeneth unto counsel is wise.   PROVERBS 12:15

Ointment and perfume rejoice the heart: so doth the sweetness of a man's friend by hearty counsel.   PROVERBS 27:9

Without counsel purposes are disappointed: but in the multitude of counsellors they are established.   PROVERBS 15:22

For whom the Lord loveth he chasteneth, and scourgeth every son whom he receiveth.
    If ye endure chastening, God dealeth with you as with sons; for what son is he whom the father chasteneth not?
                                          HEBREWS 12:6–7

A wise man will hear, and will increase learning; and a man of understanding shall attain unto wise counsels.   PROVERBS 1:5

Dear God,

I pray that I won't be too proud to
ask for help and advice from others.
Please let me be receptive to their words.
When others come to me for counsel,
give me ears to listen and the right words to respond.
Amen.

Courage

$\mathcal{Y}$ou have to accept whatever comes
and the only important thing is
that you meet it with courage,
and with the best you have to give.

ELEANOR ROOSEVELT

Only be thou strong and very courageous, that thou mayest observe to do according to all the law, which Moses my servant commanded thee: turn not from it to the right hand or to the left, that thou mayest prosper whithersoever thou goest.

JOSHUA 1:7

Wait on the LORD: be of good courage, and he shall strengthen thine heart: wait, I say, on the LORD.   PSALM 27:14

Be of good courage,
and he shall strengthen your heart,
all ye that hope in the Lord.

PSALM 31:24

For God hath not given us the spirit of fear; but of power, and of love, and of a sound mind.   2 TIMOTHY 1:7

So that we may boldly say, The Lord is my helper, and I will not fear what man shall do unto me.   HEBREWS 13:6

In the fear of the LORD is strong confidence: and his children shall have a place of refuge.   PROVERBS 14:26

Watch ye, stand fast in the faith, quit you like men, be strong.

1 CORINTHIANS 16:13

Only let your conversation be as it becometh the gospel of Christ: that whether I come and see you, or else be absent, I may hear of your affairs, that ye stand fast in one spirit, with one mind striving together for the faith of the gospel;

And in nothing terrified by your adversaries: which is to them an evident token of perdition, but to you of salvation, and that of God.   PHILIPPIANS 1:27–28

And now, little children, abide in him; that, when he shall appear, we may have confidence, and not be ashamed before him at his coming.   1 JOHN 2:28

The wicked flee when no man pursueth: but the righteous are bold as a lion.   PROVERBS 28:1

Having therefore, brethren, boldness to enter into the holiest by the blood of Jesus.   HEBREWS 10:19

In whom we have boldness and access with confidence by the faith of him.   EPHESIANS 3:12

Father,

forgive me when I'm fearful.
I know that You are bigger than anything
I may encounter in life.
Remind me that You have laid out my future,
and You already know what is going to happen.
I confess my apprehension.
Amen.

Diligence

When I stand before God
at the end of my life,
I would hope that I would not have a single bit of
talent left and could say,
"I used everything you gave me."

ERMA BOMBECK

I call to remembrance my song in the night: I commune with mine own heart: and my spirit made diligent search.

PSALM 77:6

But take diligent heed to do the commandment and the law, which Moses the servant of the LORD charged you, to love the LORD your God, and to walk in all his ways, and to keep his commandments, and to cleave unto him, and to serve him with all your heart and with all your soul.   JOSHUA 22:5

Keep thy heart with all diligence; for out of it are the issues of life.   PROVERBS 4:23

Therefore, as ye abound in every thing, in faith, and utterance, and knowledge, and in all diligence, and in your love to us, see that ye abound in this grace also.   2 CORINTHIANS 8:7

Labour not for the meat which perisheth, but for that meat which endureth unto everlasting life, which the Son of man shall give unto you: for him hath God the Father sealed.

JOHN 6:27

He becometh poor that dealeth with a slack hand: but the hand of the diligent maketh rich.   PROVERBS 10:4

The soul of the sluggard desireth, and hath nothing: but the soul of the diligent shall be made fat.   PROVERBS 13:4

Whatsoever is commanded by the God of heaven, let it be diligently done for the house of the God of heaven: for why should there be wrath against the realm of the king and his sons?

EZRA 7:23

And beside this, giving all diligence, add to your faith virtue; and to virtue knowledge;

And to knowledge temperance; and to temperance patience; and to patience godliness;

And to godliness brotherly kindness; and to brotherly kindness charity. . . .

Wherefore the rather, brethren, give diligence to make your calling and election sure: for if ye do these things, ye shall never fall.   2 PETER 1:5–7, 10

But ye, brethren,
be not weary in well doing.

2 THESSALONIANS 3:13

I must work the works of him that sent me, while it is day: the night cometh, when no man can work.   JOHN 9:4

Or he that exhorteth, on exhortation: he that giveth, let him do it with simplicity; he that ruleth, with diligence; he that sheweth mercy, with cheerfulness.   ROMANS 12:8

Therefore, my beloved brethren, be ye stedfast, unmoveable, always abounding in the work of the Lord, forasmuch as ye know that your labour is not in vain in the Lord.

1 CORINTHIANS 15:58

Wherefore, beloved, seeing that ye look for such things, be diligent that ye may be found of him in peace, without spot, and blameless.   2 PETER 3:14

Behold that which I have seen: it is good and comely for one to eat and to drink, and to enjoy the good of all his labour that he taketh under the sun all the days of his life, which God giveth him: for it is his portion.

Every man also to whom God hath given riches and wealth, and hath given him power to eat thereof, and to take his portion, and to rejoice in his labour; this is the gift of God.
                                        ECCLESIASTES 5:18–19

The thoughts of the diligent tend only to plenteousness; but of every one that is hasty only to want.   PROVERBS 21:5

And let us not be weary in well doing: for in due season we shall reap, if we faint not.   GALATIANS 6:9

Much food is in the tillage of the poor: but there is that is destroyed for want of judgment.   PROVERBS 13:23

Thank You

for opportunities, Jesus.
Day by day through study and work,
help me to reach higher levels of character.
In my climb, Lord, guide me to great heights.
Amen.

Discipline, Family

I can't think of anything
parents could do to children
more heartless than
failing to discipline.

JANETTE OKE

One that ruleth well his own house, having his children in subjection with all gravity;

(For if a man know not how to rule his own house, how
shall he take care of the church of God?)   1 TIMOTHY 3:4–5

And, ye fathers, provoke not your children to wrath: but bring
them up in the nurture and admonition of the Lord.

EPHESIANS 6:4

Correct thy son, and he shall give thee rest; yea, he shall give
delight unto thy soul.   PROVERBS 29:17

He that spareth his rod hateth his son: but he that loveth him
chasteneth him betimes.   PROVERBS 13:24

Foolishness is bound in the heart of a child; but the rod of correction shall drive it far from him.   PROVERBS 22:15

Now, lo, if he beget a son, that seeth all his father's sins which
he hath done, and considereth, and doeth not such like,

That hath not eaten upon the mountains, neither hath lifted up his eyes to the idols of the house of Israel, hath not
defiled his neighbour's wife,

Neither hath oppressed any, hath not withholden the pledge,
neither hath spoiled by violence, but hath given his bread to the
hungry, and hath covered the naked with a garment,

That hath taken off his hand from the poor, that hath not
received usury nor increase, hath executed my judgments, hath
walked in my statutes; he shall not die for the iniquity of his
father, he shall surely live.   EZEKIEL 18:14–17

Chasten thy son while there is hope, and let not thy soul spare for his crying.   PROVERBS 19:18

Withhold not correction from the child: for if thou beatest him with the rod, he shall not die.

   Thou shalt beat him with the rod, and shalt deliver his soul from hell.   PROVERBS 23:13–14

Fathers, provoke not
your children to anger,
lest they be discouraged.

COLOSSIANS 3:21

Even a child is known by his doings, whether his work be pure, and whether it be right.   PROVERBS 20:11

God,
give me the wisdom to discipline my children.
Thank You for lovingly disciplining me, Lord.
Help me to learn from my mistakes so that
I can be conformed to Your image.
Amen.

Discipline, God's

God has to punish
His children from time to time
and it is the very
demonstration of His love.

ELISABETH ELLIOT

O Lord, rebuke me not in thine anger, neither chasten me in thy hot displeasure.   PSALM 6:1

As many as I love, I rebuke and chasten: be zealous therefore, and repent.   REVELATION 3:19

For whom the Lord
loveth he correcteth;
even as a father the son
in whom he delighteth.

PROVERBS 3:12

Thou shalt also consider in thine heart, that, as a man chasteneth his son, so the LORD thy God chasteneth thee.
                                    DEUTERONOMY 8:5

For if we would judge ourselves, we should not be judged.
    But when we are judged, we are chastened of the Lord, that we should not be condemned with the world.
                                    1 CORINTHIANS 11:31–32

Behold, happy is the man whom God correcteth: therefore despise not thou the chastening of the Almighty:
    For he maketh sore, and bindeth up: he woundeth, and his hands make whole.   JOB 5:17–18

The LORD hath chasteneth me sore: but he hath not given me over unto death.   PSALM 118:18

And ye have forgotten the exhortation which speaketh unto you as unto children, My son, despise not thou the chastening of the Lord, nor faint when thou art rebuked of him:

For whom the Lord loveth he chasteneth, and scourgeth every son whom he receiveth.

If ye endure chastening, God dealeth with you as with sons; for what son is he whom the father chasteneth not?

But if ye be without chastisement, whereof all are partakers, then are ye bastards, and not sons.   HEBREWS 12:5–8

For the commandment is a lamp; and the law is light; and reproofs of instruction are the way of life.   PROVERBS 6:23

Blessed is the man whom thou chastenest, O LORD, and teachest him out of thy law;

That thou mayest give him rest from the days of adversity, until the pit be digged for the wicked.   PSALM 94:12–13

Now no chastening for the present seemeth to be joyous, but grievous: nevertheless afterward it yieldeth the peaceable fruit of righteousness unto them which are exercised thereby.
                                                HEBREWS 12:11

Thank You, God,

for Your correction when I make the wrong choices.
Discipline hurts, but I pray
that it will teach me to stay close to You
and not wander out on my own.
May I learn to obey You.
Amen.

Duty

Laziness may appear attractive,
but work gives satisfaction.

ANNE FRANK

Let us hear the conclusion of the whole matter: Fear God, and keep his commandments: for this is the whole duty of man.

ECCLESIASTES 12:13

And if it seem evil unto you to serve the LORD, choose you this day whom ye will serve. . .but as for me and my house, we will serve the LORD.   JOSHUA 24:15

If ye be willing and obedient,
ye shall eat the good of the land.

ISAIAH 1:19

Now therefore, if ye will obey my voice indeed, and keep my covenant, then ye shall be a peculiar treasure unto me above all people: for all the earth is mine.   EXODUS 19:5

Thou shalt keep therefore his statutes, and his commandments, which I command thee this day, that it may go well with thee, and with thy children after thee, and that thou mayest prolong thy days upon the earth, which the LORD thy God giveth thee, for ever.   DEUTERONOMY 4:40

And he sought God in the days of Zechariah, who had understanding in the visions of God: and as long as he sought the LORD, God made him to prosper.   2 CHRONICLES 26:5

When a man's ways please the LORD, he maketh even his enemies to be at peace with him.   PROVERBS 16:7

Save when there shall be no poor among you; for the LORD
shall greatly bless thee in the land which the LORD thy God
giveth thee for an inheritance to possess it:
     Only if thou carefully hearken unto the voice of the LORD
thy God, to observe to do all these commandments which I
command thee this day.   DEUTERONOMY 15:4–5

If they obey and serve him, they shall spend their days in prosperity, and their years in pleasures.   JOB 36:11

And why call ye me, Lord, Lord, and do not the things which
I say?   LUKE 6:46

And shewing mercy unto thousands of them that love me, and
keep my commandments.   EXODUS 20:6

Observe and hear all these words which I command thee, that
it may go well with thee, and with thy children after thee for
ever, when thou doest that which is good and right in the sight
of the LORD thy God.   DEUTERONOMY 12:28

See, I have set before thee this day life and good, and death
and evil;
     In that I command thee this day to love the LORD thy God,
to walk in his ways, and to keep his commandments and his
statutes and his judgments, that thou mayest live and multiply:
and the LORD thy God shall bless thee in the land whither thou
goest to possess it.   DEUTERONOMY 30:15–16

And ye shall be hated of all men for my name's sake: but he that endureth to the end shall be saved.   MATTHEW 10:22

Father,
help me to see today how I can be useful.
Then give me the strength to walk into
the opportunities You have set before me.
Amen.

Encouragement

(U)hat men and women need
is encouragement. . . .
Instead of always harping on
a man's faults,
tell him of his virtues.
Try to pull him out of his
rut of bad habits.

ELEANOR H. PORTER

But exhort one another daily, while it is called Today; lest any of you be hardened through the deceitfulness of sin.

HEBREWS 3:13

Confirming the souls of the disciples, and exhorting them to continue in the faith, and that we must through much tribulation enter into the kingdom of God.   ACTS 14:22

Bear ye one another's burdens,
and so fulfil the law of Christ.

GALATIANS 6:2

Holding fast the faithful word as he hath been taught, that he may be able by sound doctrine both to exhort and to convince the gainsayers.   TITUS 1:9

Not forsaking the assembling of ourselves together, as the manner of some is; but exhorting one another: and so much the more, as ye see the day approaching.   HEBREWS 10:25

I can do all things through Christ which strengtheneth me.

PHILIPPIANS 4:13

He giveth power to the faint; and to them that have no might he increaseth strength.   ISAIAH 40:29

Therefore, brethren, stand fast, and hold the traditions which ye have been taught, whether by word, or our epistle.

Now our Lord Jesus Christ himself, and God, even our Father, which hath loved us, and hath given us everlasting consolation and good hope through grace,

Comfort your hearts, and stablish you in every good word and work. 2 THESSALONIANS 2:15–17

And when they bring you unto the synagogues, and unto magistrates, and powers, take ye no thought how or what thing ye shall answer, or what ye shall say:

For the Holy Ghost shall teach you in the same hour what ye ought to say. LUKE 12:11–12

Wherefore comfort yourselves together, and edify one another, even as also ye do. 1 THESSALONIANS 5:11

And whether we be afflicted, it is for your consolation and salvation, which is effectual in the enduring of the same sufferings which we also suffer: or whether we be comforted, it is for your consolation and salvation. 2 CORINTHIANS 1:6

All scripture is given by inspiration of God, and is profitable for doctrine, for reproof, for correction, for instruction in righteousness. 2 TIMOTHY 3:16

Brethren, if any of you do err from the truth, and one convert him;

Let him know, that he which converteth the sinner from the error of his way shall save a soul from death, and shall hide a multitude of sins. JAMES 5:19–20

Ye are witnesses, and God also, how holily and justly and unblameably we behaved ourselves among you that believe:

As ye know how we exhorted and comforted and charged every one of you, as a father doth his children,

That ye would walk worthy of God, who hath called you unto his kingdom and glory.

For this cause also thank we God without ceasing, because, when ye received the word of God which ye heard of us, ye received it not as the word of men, but as it is in truth, the word of God, which effectually worketh also in you that believe.

1 THESSALONIANS 2:10–13

Look not every man on his own things, but every man also on the things of others.   PHILIPPIANS 2:4

Lord Jesus,
*thank You for the encouraging words
that others have for me.
I pray that I will be
an encouragement to others as well.
Amen.*

Eternity

Redeemed,
how I love to proclaim it!
His child, and forever, I am.

FANNY CROSBY

In my Father's house are many mansions: if it were not so, I would have told you. I go to prepare a place for you.

And if I go and prepare a place for you, I will come again, and receive you unto myself; that where I am, there ye may be also.   JOHN 14:2–3

Henceforth there is laid up for me a crown of righteousness, which the Lord, the righteous judge, shall give me at that day: and not to me only, but unto all them also that love his appearing.   2 TIMOTHY 4:8

He that soweth to the Spirit
shall of the Spirit reap
life everlasting.

GALATIANS 6:8

And I saw a new heaven and a new earth: for the first heaven and the first earth were passed away; and there was no more sea.

And I John saw the holy city, new Jerusalem, coming down from God out of heaven, prepared as a bride adorned for her husband.   REVELATION 21:1–2

And I give unto them eternal life; and they shall never perish, neither shall any man pluck them out of my hand.   JOHN 10:28

And he saith unto them, Ye shall drink indeed of my cup, and be baptized with the baptism that I am baptized with: but to sit on my right hand, and on my left, is not mine to give, but it shall be given to them for whom it is prepared of my Father.

MATTHEW 20:23

He that loveth his life shall lose it; and he that hateth his life in this world shall keep it unto life eternal.   JOHN 12:25

For the wages of sin is death; but the gift of God is eternal life through Jesus Christ our Lord.   ROMANS 6:23

For we know that if our earthly house of this tabernacle were dissolved, we have a building of God, an house not made with hands, eternal in the heavens.   2 CORINTHIANS 5:1

Behold, I shew you a mystery; We shall not all sleep, but we shall all be changed,

In a moment, in the twinkling of an eye, at the last trump: for the trumpet shall sound, and the dead shall be raised incorruptible, and we shall be changed.

For this corruptible must put on incorruption, and this mortal must put on immortality.

So when this corruptible shall have put on incorruption, and this mortal shall have put on immortality, then shall be brought to pass the saying that is written, Death is swallowed up in victory.   1 CORINTHIANS 15:51–54

Nevertheless we, according to his promise, look for new heavens and a new earth, wherein dwelleth righteousness.

2 PETER 3:13

And when the chief Shepherd shall appear, ye shall receive a crown of glory that fadeth not away.   1 PETER 5:4

And many of them that sleep in the dust of the earth shall awake, some to everlasting life, and some to shame and ever-lasting contempt.   DANIEL 12:2

And the world passeth away,
and the lust thereof:
but he that doeth the will
of God abideth for ever.

1 JOHN 2:17

Jesus said unto her, I am the resurrection, and the life: he that believeth in me, though he were dead, yet shall he live:
    And whosoever liveth and believeth in me shall never die. Believest thou this?   JOHN 11:25–26

Search the scriptures; for in them ye think ye have eternal life: and they are they which testify of me.   JOHN 5:39

God. . .will render to every man according to his deeds:
    To them who by patient continuance in well doing seek for glory and honour and immortality, eternal life.
          ROMANS 2:5–7

Labour not for the meat which perisheth, but for that meat which endureth unto everlasting life, which the Son of man shall give unto you: for him hath God the Father sealed.

JOHN 6:27

But if the Spirit of him that raised up Jesus from the dead dwell in you, he that raised up Christ from the dead shall also quicken your mortal bodies by his Spirit that dwelleth in you.

ROMANS 8:11

And there shall be no night there; and they need no candle, neither light of the sun; for the Lord God giveth them light: and they shall reign for ever and ever.   REVELATION 22:5

Blessed be the God and Father of our Lord Jesus Christ, which according to his abundant mercy hath begotten us again unto a lively hope by the resurrection of Jesus Christ from the dead,

To an inheritance incorruptible, and undefiled, and that fadeth not away, reserved in heaven for you,

Who are kept by the power of God through faith unto salvation ready to be revealed in the last time.   1 PETER 1:3–5

Therefore are they before the throne of God, and serve him day and night in his temple: and he that sitteth on the throne shall dwell among them.

They shall hunger no more, neither thirst any more; neither shall the sun light on them, nor any heat.

For the Lamb which is in the midst of the throne shall feed them, and shall lead them unto living fountains of waters: and God shall wipe away all tears from their eyes.

REVELATION 7:15–17

Verily, verily, I say unto you, He that heareth my word, and believeth on him that sent me, hath everlasting life, and shall not come into condemnation; but is passed from death unto life.

JOHN 5:24

Lord God,

*I feel so special when I think that You are
preparing a place in heaven for me.
To be considered Your child is overwhelming,
as You have chosen me to be a part of Your family.
I long to be in Your presence,
laying my crown at Your feet,
and worshipping You forever.
Amen.*

Faith

Faith sees the invisible,
believes the unbelievable,
and receives the impossible.

CORRIE TEN BOOM

Ask in faith, nothing wavering. For he that wavereth is like a wave of the sea driven with the wind and tossed.   JAMES 1:6

And the Lord said, If ye had faith as a grain of mustard seed, ye might say unto this sycamine tree, Be thou plucked up by the root, and be thou planted in the sea; and it should obey you.

LUKE 17:6

Now faith is the substance of things hoped for,
the evidence of things not seen.

HEBREWS 11:1

Whom having not seen, ye love; in whom, though now ye see him not, yet believing, ye rejoice with joy unspeakable and full of glory.   1 PETER 1:8

As soon as Jesus heard the word that was spoken, he saith unto the ruler of the synagogue, Be not afraid, only believe.

MARK 5:36

And he said to the woman, Thy faith hath saved thee; go in peace.   LUKE 7:50

For ye are all the children of God by faith in Christ Jesus.

GALATIANS 3:26

But as many as received him, to them gave he power to become the sons of God, even to them that believe on his name.

JOHN 1:12

He that believeth and is baptized shall be saved; but he that believeth not shall be damned.   MARK 16:16

That Christ may dwell in your hearts by faith; that ye, being rooted and grounded in love,

May be able to comprehend with all saints what is the breadth, and length, and depth, and height;

And to know the love of Christ, which passeth knowledge, that ye might be filled with all the fulness of God.

EPHESIANS 3:17–19

Jesus said unto him, If thou canst believe, all things are possible to him that believeth.   MARK 9:23

It is written in the prophets, And they shall be all taught of God. Every man therefore that hath heard, and hath learned of the Father, cometh unto me.   JOHN 6:45

That your faith should not stand in the wisdom of men, but in the power of God.   1 CORINTHIANS 2:5

Watch ye, stand fast in the faith, quit you like men, be strong.

1 CORINTHIANS 16:13

That if thou shalt confess with thy mouth the Lord Jesus, and shalt believe in thine heart that God hath raised him from the dead, thou shalt be saved.   ROMANS 10:9

And Jesus answering saith unto them, Have faith in God.

For verily I say unto you, That whosoever shall say unto this mountain, Be thou removed, and be thou cast into the sea; and shall not doubt in his heart, but shall believe that those things which he saith shall come to pass; he shall have whatsoever he saith.   MARK 11:22–23

For by grace are ye saved through faith; and that not of yourselves: it is the gift of God.   EPHESIANS 2:8

For we walk by faith,
          not by sight.

2 CORINTHIANS 5:7

Jesus saith unto him, Thomas, because thou hast seen me, thou hast believed: blessed are they that have not seen, and yet have believed.   JOHN 20:29

But without faith it is impossible to please him: for he that cometh to God must believe that he is, and that he is a rewarder of them that diligently seek him.   HEBREWS 11:6

Let us draw near with a true heart in full assurance of faith, having our hearts sprinkled from an evil conscience, and our bodies washed with pure water.   HEBREWS 10:22

Jesus answered and said unto them, This is the work of God, that ye believe on him whom he hath sent.   JOHN 6:29

He that believeth on the Son of God hath the witness in himself: he that believeth not God hath made him a liar; because he believeth not the record that God gave of his Son.
                                                    1 JOHN 5:10

As ye have therefore received Christ Jesus the Lord, so walk ye in him.   COLOSSIANS 2:6–7

Behold, I stand at the door, and knock: if any man hear my voice, and open the door, I will come in to him, and will sup with him, and he with me.   REVELATION 3:20

Jesus saith unto her, Said I not unto thee, that, if thou wouldest believe, thou shouldest see the glory of God?   JOHN 11:40

The life which I now live in the flesh I live by the faith of the Son of God, who loved me, and gave himself for me.
                                                GALATIANS 2:20

Father,

please help me to be a woman of faith,
believing that You will work all details out in my life.
Let me not rely on tangible, explainable things,
but to remember that You are in control of everything—
known and unknown.

Faithfulness
of God

God's designs regarding you,
and His methods of bringing about these designs,
are infinitely wise.

MADAME GUYON

And we know that all things work together for good to them that love God, to them who are the called according to his purpose. ROMANS 8:28

And the heavens shall praise thy wonders, O LORD: thy faithfulness also in the congregation of the saints. PSALM 89:5

A faithful man shall abound with blessings: but he that maketh haste to be rich shall not be innocent. PROVERBS 28:20

In hope of eternal life, which God, that cannot lie, promised before the world began. TITUS 1:2

Who then is a faithful and wise servant, whom his lord hath made ruler over his household, to give them meat in due season?

Blessed is that servant, whom his lord when he cometh shall find so doing.

Verily I say unto you, That he shall make him ruler over all his goods. MATTHEW 24:45–47

Therefore thus saith the Lord GOD, Behold, I lay in Zion for a foundation a stone, a tried stone, a precious corner stone, a sure foundation: he that believeth shall not make haste.

ISAIAH 28:16

The Lord is not slack concerning his promise, as some men count slackness; but is longsuffering to us-ward, not willing that any should perish, but that all should come to repentance.

2 PETER 3:9

Be thou faithful unto death, and I will give thee a crown of life. REVELATION 2:10

(For the LORD thy God is a merciful God;) he will not forsake thee, neither destroy thee, nor forget the covenant of thy fathers which he sware unto them.   DEUTERONOMY 4:31

Let us hold fast the profession of our faith without wavering; (for he is faithful that promised).   HEBREWS 10:23

If we believe not,
yet he abideth faithful:
he cannot deny himself.

2 TIMOTHY 2:13

God is not a man, that he should lie; neither the son of man, that he should repent: hath he said, and shall he not do it? Or hath he spoken, and shall he not make it good?
                                                  NUMBERS 23:19

Blessed be the LORD, that hath given rest unto his people Israel, according to all that he promised: there hath not failed one word of all his good promise, which he promised by the hand of Moses his servant.   1 KINGS 8:56

O love the LORD, all ye his saints: for the LORD preserveth the faithful, and plentifully rewardeth the proud doer.
                                                  PSALM 31:23

Know therefore that the LORD thy God, he is God, the faithful God, which keepeth covenant and mercy with them that love him and keep his commandments to a thousand generations.

DEUTERONOMY 7:9

Thank You, Lord,
for remaining steadfast.
Nothing else in my life is as sure as You.
I am grateful that You will never leave me,
regardless of what I do.
I love You, Lord!
Amen.

Fearing God

R everence for the Lord
is the beginning of wisdom.

ELISABETH ELLIOT

And fear not them which kill the body, but are not able to kill the soul: but rather fear him which is able to destroy both soul and body in hell.   MATTHEW 10:28

Moreover thou shalt provide out of all the people able men, such as fear God, men of truth, hating covetousness; and place such over them, to be rulers of thousands, and rulers of hundreds, rulers of fifties, and rulers of tens.   EXODUS 18:21

The fear of the LORD is the beginning of knowledge: but fools despise wisdom and instruction.   PROVERBS 1:7

Saying with a loud voice, Fear God, and give glory to him; for the hour of his judgment is come: and worship him that made heaven, and earth, and the sea, and the fountains of waters.
                                    REVELATION 14:7

O that there were such an heart in them, that they would fear me, and keep all my commandments always, that it might be well with them, and with their children for ever!
                                    DEUTERONOMY 5:29

The angel of the LORD encampeth round about them that fear him, and delivereth them.   PSALM 34:7

Thou believest that there is one God; thou doest well: the devils also believe, and tremble.   JAMES 2:19

Only fear the LORD, and serve him in truth with all your heart: for consider how great things he hath done for you.
                                    1 SAMUEL 12:24

A wise man feareth, and departeth from evil: but the fool rageth, and is confident.   PROVERBS 14:16

Wherefore we receiving a kingdom which cannot be moved, let us have grace, whereby we may serve God acceptably with reverence and godly fear:

For our God is a consuming fire.   HEBREWS 12:28–29

He will fulfil the desire
of them that fear him:
he also will hear their cry,
and will save them.

PSALM 145:19

Men do therefore fear him: he respecteth not any that are wise of heart.   JOB 37:24

Then they that feared the LORD spake often one to another: and the LORD hearkened, and heard it, and a book of remembrance was written before him for them that feared the LORD, and that thought upon his name.   MALACHI 3:16

Wherefore, my beloved, as ye have always obeyed, not as in my presence only, but now much more in my absence, work out your own salvation with fear and trembling.   PHILIPPIANS 2:12

The secret of the LORD is with them that fear him; and he will shew them his covenant.   PSALM 25:14

Having therefore these promises, dearly beloved, let us cleanse ourselves from all filthiness of the flesh and spirit, perfecting holiness in the fear of God.   2 CORINTHIANS 7:1

The fear of the LORD is to hate evil: pride, and arrogancy, and the evil way, and the froward mouth, do I hate.   PROVERBS 8:13

Let us hear the conclusion of the whole matter: Fear God, and keep his commandments: for this is the whole duty of man.
ECCLESIASTES 12:13

Fear ye not me? saith the LORD: will ye not tremble at my presence, which have placed the sand for the bound of the sea by a perpetual decree, that it cannot pass it: and though the waves thereof toss themselves, yet can they not prevail; though they roar, yet can they not pass over it?   JEREMIAH 5:22

Serve the LORD with fear, and rejoice with trembling.
PSALM 2:11

Lord God,
You are holy.
You can control anything with a mere whisper.
Yet You love me and are patient with me.
Thank You, Father!
Amen.

Forgiveness

If the wounds of millions
are to be healed,
what other way is there except
through forgiveness?

CATHERINE MARSHALL

And be ye kind one to another, tenderhearted, forgiving one another, even as God for Christ's sake hath forgiven you.

EPHESIANS 4:32

Forbearing one another, and forgiving one another, if any man have a quarrel against any: even as Christ forgave you, so also do ye. COLOSSIANS 3:13

Not rendering evil for evil, or railing for railing: but contrariwise blessing; knowing that ye are thereunto called, that ye should inherit a blessing. 1 PETER 3:9

For if ye forgive men their trespasses, your heavenly Father will also forgive you:

But if ye forgive not men their trespasses, neither will your Father forgive your trespasses. MATTHEW 6:14–15

Then came Peter to him, and said, Lord, how oft shall my brother sin against me, and I forgive him? till seven times?

Jesus saith unto him, I say not unto thee, Until seven times: but, Until seventy times seven. MATTHEW 18:21–22

Take heed to yourselves: If thy brother trespass against thee, rebuke him; and if he repent, forgive him.

And if he trespass against thee seven times in a day, and seven times in a day turn again to thee, saying, I repent; thou shalt forgive him. LUKE 17:3–4

And forgive us our sins; for we also forgive every one that is indebted to us. And lead us not into temptation; but deliver us from evil. LUKE 11:4

And when ye stand praying, forgive, if ye have ought against any: that your Father also which is in heaven may forgive you your trespasses.

But if ye do not forgive, neither will your Father which is in heaven forgive your trespasses.   MARK 11:25–26

The discretion of a man deferreth his anger; and it is his glory to pass over a transgression.   PROVERBS 19:11

And forgive us our debts,
as we forgive our debtors.

MATTHEW 6:12

And said unto Simon, Seest thou this woman? . . . she hath washed my feet with tears, and wiped them with the hairs of her head. . .

[and] hath not ceased to kiss my feet. . . .

this woman hath anointed my feet with ointment.

Wherefore I say unto thee, Her sins, which are many, are forgiven; for she loved much: but to whom little is forgiven, the same loveth little.

He said unto her, Thy sins are forgiven.   LUKE 7:44–48

For thou, Lord, art good, and ready to forgive; and plenteous in mercy unto all them that call upon thee.   PSALM 86:5

But I say unto you, That ye resist not evil: but whosoever shall smite thee on thy right cheek, turn to him the other also.

And if any man will sue thee at the law, and take away thy coat, let him have thy cloke also.

And whosoever shall compel thee to go a mile, go with him twain.   MATTHEW 5:39–41

If my people, which are called by my name, shall humble themselves, and pray, and seek my face, and turn from their wicked ways; then will I hear from heaven, and will forgive their sin, and will heal their land.   2 CHRONICLES 7:14

Judge not, and ye shall not be judged: condemn not, and ye shall not be condemned: forgive, and ye shall be forgiven.

LUKE 6:37

Dear God,

forgive me for sinning against You.
It hurts me to know that I've failed You,
the One who has given me the gift of new life.
When others wound me,
may I extend to them the same forgiveness
that You grant to me.

Friendship

y friends are my estate.

EMILY DICKINSON

Iron sharpeneth iron; so a man sharpeneth the countenance of his friend.   PROVERBS 27:17

Which of you shall have a friend, and shall go unto him at midnight, and say unto him, Friend, lend me three loaves;
     For a friend of mine in his journey is come to me, and I have nothing to set before him?
     And he from within shall answer and say. . .I cannot rise and give thee.
     I say unto you, Though he will not rise and give him, because he is his friend, yet because of his importunity he will rise and give him as many as he needeth.   LUKE 11:5–8

A friend loveth at all times.   PROVERBS 17:17

A man that hath friends must shew himself friendly: and there is a friend that sticketh closer than a brother.   PROVERBS 18:24

To him that is afflicted pity should be shewed from his friend; but he forsaketh the fear of the Almighty.   JOB 6:14

Faithful are the wounds of a friend.   PROVERBS 27:6

Whosoever therefore will be a friend of the world is the enemy of God.   JAMES 4:4

Heavenly Father,
I praise You for the friends You've provided for me.
Bless them for their investment in my life.

Generosity

It's not how much we give
but how much love
we put into giving.

MOTHER TERESA

He hath dispersed, he hath given to the poor; his righteousness endureth for ever; his horn shall be exalted with honour.

PSALM 112:9

Charge them that are rich in this world, that they be not high-minded, nor trust in uncertain riches, but in the living God, who giveth us richly all things to enjoy;

That they do good, that they be rich in good works, ready to distribute, willing to communicate.   1 TIMOTHY 6:17–18

But when thou makest a feast, call the poor, the maimed, the lame, the blind:

And thou shalt be blessed; for they cannot recompense thee: for thou shalt be recompensed at the resurrection of the just.

LUKE 14:13–14

Withhold not good from them to whom it is due, when it is in the power of thine hand to do it.

Say not unto thy neighbour, Go, and come again, and to-morrow I will give; when thou hast it by thee.

PROVERBS 3:27–28

He answereth and saith unto them, He that hath two coats, let him impart to him that hath none; and he that hath meat, let him do likewise.   LUKE 3:11

If a brother or sister be naked, and destitute of daily food,

And one of you say unto them, Depart in peace, be ye warmed and filled; notwithstanding ye give them not those things which are needful to the body; what doth it profit?

JAMES 2:15–16

Therefore when thou doest thine alms, do not sound a trumpet before thee, as the hypocrites do in the synagogues and in the streets, that they may have glory of men. Verily I say unto you, They have their reward.

But when thou doest alms, let not thy left hand know what thy right hand doeth:

That thine alms may be in secret: and thy Father which seeth in secret himself shall reward thee openly.

MATTHEW 6:2–4

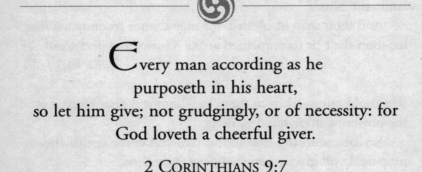

Every man according as he
purposeth in his heart,
so let him give; not grudgingly, or of necessity: for
God loveth a cheerful giver.

2 CORINTHIANS 9:7

Blessed is he that considereth the poor: the LORD will deliver him in time of trouble.

The LORD will preserve him, and keep him alive; and he shall be blessed upon the earth: and thou wilt not deliver him unto the will of his enemies.   PSALM 41:1–2

And if thy brother be waxen poor, and fallen in decay with thee; then thou shalt relieve him: yea, though he be a stranger, or a sojourner; that he may live with thee.   LEVITICUS 25:35

He that despiseth his neighbour sinneth: but he that hath mercy on the poor, happy is he.   PROVERBS 14:21

If any man or woman that believeth have widows, let them relieve them, and let not the church be charged; that it may relieve them that are widows indeed.   1 TIMOTHY 5:16

And he saw also a certain poor widow casting in thither two mites.

And he said, Of a truth I say unto you, that this poor widow hath cast in more than they all:

For all these have of their abundance cast in unto the offerings of God: but she of her penury hath cast in all the living that she had.   LUKE 21:2–4

Then shall the King say unto them on his right hand, Come, ye blessed of my Father, inherit the kingdom prepared for you from the foundation of the world:

For I was an hungred, and ye gave me meat: I was thirsty, and ye gave me drink: I was a stranger, and ye took me in:

Naked, and ye clothed me: I was sick, and ye visited me: I was in prison, and ye came unto me.

Then shall the righteous answer him, saying, Lord, when saw we thee an hungred, and fed thee? or thirsty, and gave thee drink?

When saw we thee a stranger, and took thee in? or naked, and clothed thee?

Or when saw we thee sick, or in prison, and came unto thee?

And the King shall answer and say unto them, Verily I say unto you, Inasmuch as ye have done it unto one of the least of these my brethren, ye have done it unto me.

MATTHEW 25:34–40

For the poor shall never cease out of the land: therefore I command thee, saying, Thou shalt open thine hand wide unto thy brother, to thy poor, and to thy needy, in thy land.

DEUTERONOMY 15:11

Every man shall give
as he is able,
according to the blessing
of the Lord thy God which
he hath given thee.

DEUTERONOMY 16:17

Is it not to deal thy bread to the hungry, and that thou bring the poor that are cast out to thy house? when thou seest the naked, that thou cover him; and that thou hide not thyself from thine own flesh?

Then shall thy light break forth as the morning, and thine health shall spring forth speedily: and thy righteousness shall go before thee; the glory of the LORD shall be thy rearward.

ISAIAH 58:7–8

For whosoever shall give you a cup of water to drink in my name, because ye belong to Christ, verily I say unto you, he shall not lose his reward.

MARK 9:41

Give, and it shall be given unto you; good measure, pressed down, and shaken together, and running over, shall men give into your bosom. For with the same measure that ye mete withal it shall be measured to you again.   LUKE 6:38

For ye know the grace of our Lord Jesus Christ, that, though he was rich, yet for your sakes he became poor, that ye through his poverty might be rich.   2 CORINTHIANS 8:9

He that hath pity upon the poor lendeth unto the LORD; and that which he hath given will he pay him again.
                    PROVERBS 19:17

I have shewed you all things, how that so labouring ye ought to support the weak, and to remember the words of the Lord Jesus, how he said, It is more blessed to give than to receive.
                    ACTS 20:35

Father,

I want to share all of the blessings
You've given to me with others.
Loosen my grip when I grasp them too tightly.
I will experience joy when I share what I have with others.
Amen.

Gentleness

Take my heart and make it
your dwelling place
so that everyone I touch
will be touched also by you!

ALICE JOYCE DAVIDSON

Take my yoke upon you, and learn of me; for I am meek and lowly in heart: and ye shall find rest unto your souls.

MATTHEW 11:29

But the meek shall inherit the earth; and shall delight themselves in the abundance of peace.   PSALM 37:11

Now I Paul myself beseech you by the meekness and gentleness of Christ, who in presence am base among you, but being absent am bold toward you.   2 CORINTHIANS 10:1

Put them in mind to be subject to principalities and powers, to obey magistrates, to be ready to every good work,

To speak evil of no man, to be no brawlers, but gentle, shewing all meekness unto all men.   TITUS 3:1–2

He shall feed his flock like a shepherd: he shall gather the lambs with his arm, and carry them in his bosom, and shall gently lead those that are with young.   ISAIAH 40:11

The meek will he guide in judgment: and the meek will he teach his way.   PSALM 25:9

But the fruit of the Spirit is love, joy, peace, longsuffering, gentleness, goodness, faith.   GALATIANS 5:22

The meek shall eat and be satisfied: they shall praise the LORD that seek him: your heart shall live for ever.   PSALM 22:26

For the LORD taketh pleasure in his people: he will beautify the meek with salvation.   PSALM 149:4

And the servant of the Lord must not strive; but be gentle unto all men, apt to teach, patient,

In meekness instructing those that oppose themselves; if God peradventure will give them repentance to the acknowledging of the truth;

And that they may recover themselves out of the snare of the devil, who are taken captive by him at his will.

2 TIMOTHY 2:24–26

But the wisdom that is from above is first pure, then peaceable, gentle, and easy to be intreated, full of mercy and good fruits, without partiality, and without hypocrisy.　　JAMES 3:17

The Lord lifteth up the meek:
he casteth the wicked
down to the ground.

PSALM 147:6

But we were gentle among you, even as a nurse cherisheth her children:

So being affectionately desirous of you, we were willing to have imparted unto you, not the gospel of God only, but also our own souls.　　1 THESSALONIANS 2:7–8

Thou hast also given me the shield of thy salvation: and thy gentleness hath made me great.   2 SAMUEL 22:36

Sometimes

when life gets overwhelming,
I lose patience, Father.
Help me to react with a gentle spirit.
When I choose gentleness,
my circumstances and attitude improve.
Ripen the fruit of gentleness in my life.
Amen.

God's Love

Love has its source in God,
for love is the very essence
of His being.

KAY ARTHUR

Behold, what manner of love the Father hath bestowed upon us, that we should be called the sons of God.   1 JOHN 3:1

In this was manifested the love of God toward us, because that God sent his only begotten Son into the world, that we might live through him.   1 JOHN 4:9

I will heal their backsliding, I will love them freely: for mine anger is turned away from him.   HOSEA 14:4

But as it is written, Eye hath not seen, nor ear heard, neither have entered into the heart of man, the things which God hath prepared for them that love him.   1 CORINTHIANS 2:9

For I am persuaded, that neither death, nor life, nor angels, nor principalities, nor powers, nor things present, nor things to come,
    Nor height, nor depth, nor any other creature, shall be able to separate us from the love of God, which is in Christ Jesus our Lord.   ROMANS 8:38–39

And hope maketh not ashamed; because the love of God is shed abroad in our hearts by the Holy Ghost which is given unto us.   ROMANS 5:5

And we have known and believed the love that God hath to us. God is love; and he that dwelleth in love dwelleth in God, and God in him.   1 JOHN 4:16

For God so loved the world, that he gave his only begotten Son, that whosoever believeth in him should not perish, but have everlasting life.   JOHN 3:16

The LORD preserveth all them that love him.

PSALM 145:20

But God commendeth his love toward us, in that, while we were yet sinners, Christ died for us. ROMANS 5:8

Herein is love,
not that we loved God,
but that he loved us,
and sent his Son to be
the propitiation for our sins.

1 JOHN 4:10

For the Father himself loveth you, because ye have loved me, and have believed that I came out from God. JOHN 16:27

But if any man love God, the same is known of him.

1 CORINTHIANS 8:3

Take good heed therefore unto yourselves, that ye love the LORD your God. JOSHUA 23:11

As the Father hath loved me, so have I loved you: continue ye in my love. JOHN 15:9

Know therefore that the Lord thy God, he is God, the faithful God, which keepeth covenant and mercy with them that love him and keep his commandments to a thousand generations.

DEUTERONOMY 7:9

And Jesus answered him, The first of all the commandments is, Hear, O Israel; The Lord our God is one Lord:

And thou shalt love the Lord thy God with all thy heart, and with all thy soul, and with all thy mind, and with all thy strength: this is the first commandment.

And the second is like, namely this, Thou shalt love thy neighbour as thyself. There is none other commandment greater than these. MARK 12:29–31

The LORD hath appeared of old unto me, saying, Yea, I have loved thee with an everlasting love: therefore with lovingkindness have I drawn thee. JEREMIAH 31:3

That Christ may dwell in your hearts by faith; that ye, being rooted and grounded in love,

May be able to comprehend with all saints what is the breadth, and length, and depth, and height;

And to know the love of Christ, which passeth knowledge, that ye might be filled with all the fulness of God.

EPHESIANS 3:17–19

For God is not unrighteous to forget your work and labour of love, which ye have shewed toward his name. HEBREWS 6:10

And thou shalt love the LORD thy God with all thine heart, and with all thy soul, and with all thy might. DEUTERONOMY 6:5

Jesus said unto them, If God were your Father, ye would love me: for I proceeded forth and came from God; neither came I of myself, but he sent me.   JOHN 8:42

Love not the world, neither the things that are in the world. If any man love the world, the love of the Father is not in him.
                                          1 JOHN 2:15

I love them that love me;
and those that seek me
early shall find me.

PROVERBS 8:17

Delight thyself also in the LORD; and he shall give thee the desires of thine heart.   PSALM 37:4

And we know that all things work together for good to them that love God, to them who are the called according to his purpose.
                                          ROMANS 8:28

My son, give me thine heart, and let thine eyes observe my ways.   PROVERBS 23:26

I will declare thy name unto my brethren: in the midst of the congregation will I praise thee.   PSALM 22:22

And I have declared unto them thy name, and will declare it: that the love wherewith thou hast loved me may be in them, and I in them.   JOHN 17:26

Keep yourselves in the love of God, looking for the mercy of our Lord Jesus Christ unto eternal life.   JUDE 21

And we have known and believed the love that God hath to us. God is love; and he that dwelleth in love dwelleth in God, and God in him.

Herein is our love made perfect, that we may have boldness in the day of judgment: because as he is, so are we in this world.

There is no fear in love; but perfect love casteth out fear: because fear hath torment. He that feareth is not made perfect in love.

We love him, because he first loved us.   1 JOHN 4:16–19

He that hath my commandments, and keepeth them, he it is that loveth me: and he that loveth me shall be loved of my Father, and I will love him, and will manifest myself to him.

JOHN 14:21

Lord,
at times when I feel unlovable,
thank You for encompassing me with Your love.
Amen.

God's Provision

Lift up your eyes.
Your heavenly Father waits
to bless you in inconceivable ways to make your life
what you never dreamed
it could be.

ANNE ORTLUND

The young lions do lack, and suffer hunger: but they that seek the LORD shall not want any good thing.   PSALM 34:10

But my God shall supply all your need according to his riches in glory by Christ Jesus.   PHILIPPIANS 4:19

He hath given meat unto them that fear him.   PSALM 111:5

Therefore I say unto you, Take no thought for your life, what ye shall eat, or what ye shall drink; nor yet for your body, what ye shall put on. Is not the life more than meat, and the body than raiment?

Behold the fowls of the air: for they sow not, neither do they reap, nor gather into barns; yet your heavenly Father feedeth them. Are ye not much better than they?

Which of you by taking thought can add one cubit unto his stature?

And why take ye thought for raiment? Consider the lilies of the field, how they grow; they toil not, neither do they spin:

And yet I say unto you, That even Solomon in all his glory was not arrayed like one of these.

Wherefore, if God so clothe the grass of the field, which to day is, and tomorrow is cast into the oven, shall he not much more clothe you, O ye of little faith?

Therefore take no thought, saying, What shall we eat? or, What shall we drink? or, Wherewithal shall we be clothed?

(For after all these things do the Gentiles seek:) for your heavenly Father knoweth that ye have need of all these things.

But seek ye first the kingdom of God, and his righteousness; and all these things shall be added unto you.

MATTHEW 6:25–33

Charge them that are rich in this world, that they be not high-minded, nor trust in uncertain riches, but in the living God, who giveth us richly all things to enjoy.   1 TIMOTHY 6:17

God,

you have given me all that I need to get through this day.
I trust You to provide what I'll need tomorrow.
Please help me to refrain from
becoming envious of others' possessions,
and to trust that You will meet my needs.
Amen.

GRATITUDE

Simple gratitude helps us
experience God
at work in every moment
of every day.

HARRIET CROSBY

And he took the cup, and gave thanks, and gave it to them, saying, Drink ye all of it.   MATTHEW 26:27

I will praise thee, O LORD, with my whole heart; I will shew forth all thy marvellous works.

I will be glad and rejoice in thee: I will sing praise to thy name, O thou most High.   PSALM 9:1–2

Giving thanks always for
all things unto God and
the Father in the name of
our Lord Jesus Christ.

EPHESIANS 5:20

That I may publish with the voice of thanksgiving, and tell of all thy wondrous works.   PSALM 26:7

Blessed be the LORD, that hath given rest unto his people Israel, according to all that he promised: there hath not failed one word of all his good promise, which he promised by the hand of Moses his servant.   1 KINGS 8:56

O LORD, thou hast brought up my soul from the grave: thou hast kept me alive, that I should not go down to the pit.

PSALM 30:3

He that regardeth the day, regardeth it unto the Lord; and he that regardeth not the day, to the Lord he doth not regard it. He that eateth, eateth to the Lord, for he giveth God thanks; and he that eateth not, to the Lord he eateth not, and giveth God thanks.   ROMANS 14:6

Thou hast turned for me my mourning into dancing: thou hast put off my sackcloth, and girded me with gladness;

To the end that my glory may sing praise to thee, and not be silent. O LORD my God, I will give thanks unto thee for ever.   PSALM 30:11–12

And they, continuing daily with one accord in the temple, and breaking bread from house to house, did eat their meat with gladness and singleness of heart,

Praising God, and having favour with all the people. And the Lord added to the church daily such as should be saved.
                                                ACTS 2:46–47

I will mention the lovingkindnesses of the LORD, and the praises of the LORD, according to all that the LORD hath bestowed on us, and the great goodness toward the house of Israel, which he hath bestowed on them according to his mercies, and according to the multitude of his lovingkindnesses.   ISAIAH 63:7

Blessed be the Lord, who daily loadeth us with benefits, even the God of our salvation. Selah.   PSALM 68:19

And he took the seven loaves and the fishes, and gave thanks, and brake them, and gave to his disciples, and the disciples to the multitude.   MATTHEW 15:36

In every thing give thanks: for this is the will of God in Christ Jesus concerning you.   1 Thessalonians 5:18

Many, O LORD my God, are thy wonderful works which thou hast done, and thy thoughts which are to us-ward: they cannot be reckoned up in order unto thee: if I would declare and speak of them, they are more than can be numbered.   Psalm 40:5

I thank thee, and praise thee, O thou God of my fathers, who hast given me wisdom and might, and hast made known unto me now what we desired of thee: for thou hast now made known unto us the king's matter.   Daniel 2:23

O give thanks unto the LORD; for he is good: for his mercy endureth for ever.   Psalm 136:1

It is a good thing to give thanks unto the LORD, and to sing praises unto thy name, O most High:
    To shew forth thy lovingkindness in the morning, and thy faithfulness every night.   Psalm 92:1–2

Forgive me
for the times I'm ungrateful, Lord.
I don't intend to take Your love and blessings for granted.
Teach me to express my thanks—
to You and to others.
Amen.

Honesty

Do not do what
you would undo if caught.

LEAH ARENDT

Finally, brethren, whatsoever things are true, whatsoever things are honest, whatsoever things are just, whatsoever things are pure, whatsoever things are lovely, whatsoever things are of good report; if there be any virtue, and if there be any praise, think on these things.   PHILIPPIANS 4:8

Servants, obey in all things your masters according to the flesh; not with eyeservice, as menpleasers; but in singleness of heart, fearing God.   COLOSSIANS 3:22

Pray for us:
for we trust we have a good conscience,
in all things willing to live honestly.

HEBREWS 13:18

Then came also publicans to be baptized, and said unto him, Master, what shall we do?

And he said unto them, Exact no more than that which is appointed you.   LUKE 3:12–13

The night is far spent, the day is at hand: let us therefore cast off the works of darkness, and let us put on the armour of light.

Let us walk honestly, as in the day; not in rioting and drunkenness, not in chambering and wantonness, not in strife and envying.   ROMANS 13:12–13

Ye shall not steal, neither deal falsely, neither lie one to another.

LEVITICUS 19:11

That ye study to be quiet, and to do your own business, and to work with your own hands. . .

That ye may walk honestly toward them that are without, and that ye may have lack of nothing.

1 THESSALONIANS 4:11–12

Be of the same mind one toward another. . . .

Recompense to no man evil for evil. Provide things honest in the sight of all men.

ROMANS 12:16–17

Lie not one to another, seeing that ye have put off the old man with his deeds;

And have put on the new man, which is renewed in knowledge after the image of him that created him.

COLOSSIANS 3:9–10

He that putteth not out his money to usury, nor taketh reward against the innocent. He that doeth these things shall never be moved.

PSALM 15:5

And herein do I exercise myself, to have always a conscience void of offence toward God, and toward men. ACTS 24:16

And as ye would that men should do to you, do ye also to them likewise.

LUKE 6:31

He that hath clean hands, and a pure heart; who hath not lifted up his soul unto vanity, nor sworn deceitfully. PSALM 24:4

Thou knowest the commandments, Do not commit adultery, Do not kill, Do not steal, Do not bear false witness. . . .

MARK 10:19

He that walketh righteously, and speaketh uprightly; he that despiseth the gain of oppressions, that shaketh his hands from holding of bribes, that stoppeth his ears from hearing of blood, and shutteth his eyes from seeing evil;

He shall dwell on high: his place of defence shall be the munitions of rocks: bread shall be given him; his waters shall be sure.   ISAIAH 33:15–16

Therefore all things whatsoever ye would that men should do to you, do ye even so to them: for this is the law and the prophets.   MATTHEW 7:12

Providing for honest things,
not only in the sight of the Lord,
but also in the sight of men.

2 CORINTHIANS 8:21

Receive us; we have wronged no man, we have corrupted no man, we have defrauded no man.   2 CORINTHIANS 7:2

My righteousness I hold fast, and will not let it go: my heart
shall not reproach me so long as I live.   JOB 27:6

Heavenly Father,

it seems that it's becoming increasingly acceptable
to speak "partial truths,"
especially to avoid offending others.
But anything less than complete honesty offends You.
Help me to be a woman of honesty.
Amen.

Honor

Let our actions make us
worthy of the blessing we
have received and [pray] that
God will continue
to bless us!

DIANE ALBERS

Honour the LORD with thy substance, and with the firstfruits of all thine increase:

So shall thy barns be filled with plenty, and thy presses shall burst out with new wine.   PROVERBS 3:9–10

Children, obey your parents in the Lord: for this is right.

Honour thy father and mother; which is the first commandment with promise;

That it may be well with thee, and thou mayest live long on the earth.   EPHESIANS 6:1–3

Honour thy father and thy mother: that thy days may be long upon the land which the LORD thy God giveth thee.

EXODUS 20:12

She is more precious than rubies: and all the things thou canst desire are not to be compared unto her.

Length of days is in her right hand; and in her left hand riches and honour.   PROVERBS 3:15–16

If thou turn away thy foot from the sabbath, from doing thy pleasure on my holy day; and call the sabbath a delight, the holy of the LORD, honourable; and shalt honour him, not doing thine own ways, nor finding thine own pleasure, nor speaking thine own words:

Then shalt thou delight thyself in the LORD; and I will cause thee to ride upon the high places of the earth, and feed thee with the heritage of Jacob thy father: for the mouth of the LORD hath spoken it.   ISAIAH 58:13–14

Lord God,

I submit my all to You.
I recognize that You are the head of my life.
May my words and actions be worthy in Your sight.
Amen.

hope

Optimism is the faith
that leads to achievement.
Nothing can be done
without hope and confidence.

HELEN KELLER

Beloved, now are we the sons of God, and it doth not yet appear what we shall be: but we know that, when he shall appear, we shall be like him; for we shall see him as he is.

And every man that hath this hope in him purifieth himself, even as he is pure.   1 JOHN 3:2–3

And not only so, but we glory in tribulations also: knowing that tribulation worketh patience;

And patience, experience; and experience, hope:

And hope maketh not ashamed.   ROMANS 5:3–5

*T*hou art my hiding place and
my shield: I hope in thy word.

PSALM 119:114

The hope of the righteous shall be gladness: but the expectation of the wicked shall perish.   PROVERBS 10:28

Blessed be the God and Father of our Lord Jesus Christ, which according to his abundant mercy hath begotten us again unto a lively hope by the resurrection of Jesus Christ from the dead.   1 PETER 1:3

Blessed is the man that trusteth in the Lord, and whose hope the LORD is.   JEREMIAH 17:7

But I would not have you to be ignorant, brethren, concerning them which are asleep, that ye sorrow not, even as others which have no hope.

For if we believe that Jesus died and rose again, even so them also which sleep in Jesus will God bring with him.

1 THESSALONIANS 4:13–14

The LORD is my portion, saith my soul; therefore will I hope in him.

The LORD is good unto them that wait for him, to the soul that seeketh him.

It is good that a man should both hope and quietly wait for the salvation of the LORD.   LAMENTATIONS 3:24–26

But let us, who are of the day, be sober, putting on the breastplate of faith and love; and for an helmet, the hope of salvation.

1 THESSALONIANS 5:8

My soul fainteth for thy salvation: but I hope in thy word.

PSALM 119:81

But sanctify the Lord God in your hearts: and be ready always to give an answer to every man that asketh you a reason of the hope that is in you with meekness and fear.   1 PETER 3:15

In hope of eternal life, which God, that cannot lie, promised before the world began.   TITUS 1:2

But Christ as a son over his own house; whose house are we, if we hold fast the confidence and the rejoicing of the hope firm unto the end.   HEBREWS 3:6

For we through the Spirit wait for the hope of righteousness by faith.   GALATIANS 5:5

That by two immutable things, in which it was impossible for God to lie, we might have a strong consolation, who have fled for refuge to lay hold upon the hope set before us:

Which hope we have as an anchor of the soul, both sure and stedfast, and which entereth into that within the veil.
                                                         HEBREWS 6:18–19

Now the God of hope fill you with all joy and peace in believing, that ye may abound in hope, through the power of the Holy Ghost.   ROMANS 15:13

To whom God would make known what is the riches of the glory of this mystery among the Gentiles; which is Christ in you, the hope of glory.   COLOSSIANS 1:27

Who by him do believe in God, that raised him up from the dead, and gave him glory; that your faith and hope might be in God.   1 PETER 1:21

And have hope toward God, which they themselves also allow, that there shall be a resurrection of the dead, both of the just and unjust.   ACTS 24:15

And we desire that every one of you do shew the same diligence to the full assurance of hope unto the end.   HEBREWS 6:11

LORD, I have hoped for thy salvation, and done thy commandments.   PSALM 119:166

Who against hope believed in hope, that he might become the father of many nations, according to that which was spoken, So shall thy seed be.   ROMANS 4:18

There is one body, and one Spirit, even as ye are called in one hope of your calling.   EPHESIANS 4:4

For we are saved by hope: but hope that is seen is not hope: for what a man seeth, why doth he yet hope for?

But if we hope for that we see not, then do we with patience wait for it.   ROMANS 8:24–25

But I will hope continually,
and will yet praise thee
more and more.

PSALM 71:14

According to my earnest expectation and my hope, that in nothing I shall be ashamed, but that with all boldness, as always, so now also Christ shall be magnified in my body, whether it be by life, or by death.   PHILIPPIANS 1:20

The eyes of your understanding being enlightened; that ye may know what is the hope of his calling, and what the riches of the glory of his inheritance in the saints.   EPHESIANS 1:18

Seeing then that we have such hope, we use great plainness of speech.   2 CORINTHIANS 3:12

Remember thy word unto thy servant, upon which thou hast caused me to hope.   PSALM 119:49

Why art thou cast down, O my soul? and why art thou disquieted within me? hope thou in God: for I shall yet praise him, who is the health of my countenance, and my God.

         PSALM 42:11

For the hope which is laid up for you in heaven, whereof ye heard before in the word of the truth of the gospel.

         COLOSSIANS 1:5

Looking for that blessed hope, and the glorious appearing of the great God and our Saviour Jesus Christ.   TITUS 2:13

Now faith is the substance of things hoped for, the evidence of things not seen.   HEBREWS 11:1

For the needy shall not alway be forgotten: the expectation of the poor shall not perish for ever.   PSALM 9:18

What a joy
to hope in You, Jesus.
I know that all of Your promises are true,
and I anticipate praising You
in heaven throughout eternity.
Amen.

Hospitality

Just allow your guest
to feel at ease
because you are,
whatever the
state of your house.
This is an important element
to being a gracious host.

LINDA DAVIS ZUMBEHL

Be not forgetful to entertain strangers: for thereby some have entertained angels unawares.   HEBREWS 13:2

And if a stranger sojourn with thee in your land, ye shall not vex him.

But the stranger that dwelleth with you shall be unto you as one born among you, and thou shalt love him as thyself.   LEVITICUS 19:33–34

Distributing to the necessity of saints; given to hospitality.

ROMANS 12:13

Use hospitality one to another without grudging.   1 PETER 4:9

Be blameless, as the steward of God; not selfwilled, not soon angry, not given to wine, no striker, not given to filthy lucre;

But a lover of hospitality, a lover of good men, sober, just, holy, temperate.   TITUS 1:7–8

And thou shalt not glean thy vineyard, neither shalt thou gather every grape of thy vineyard; thou shalt leave them for the poor and stranger: I am the LORD your God.   LEVITICUS 19:10

Wisdom hath builded her house, she hath hewn out her seven pillars:

She hath killed her beasts; she hath mingled her wine; she hath also furnished her table.

She hath sent forth her maidens: she crieth upon the highest places of the city,

Whoso is simple, let him turn in hither: as for him that wanteth understanding, she saith to him,

Come, eat of my bread, and drink of the wine which I have mingled.   PROVERBS 9:1–5

He doth execute the judgment of the fatherless and widow, and loveth the stranger, in giving him food and raiment.
                    DEUTERONOMY 10:18

Then shall the King say unto them on his right hand, Come, ye blessed of my Father, inherit the kingdom prepared for you from the foundation of the world:

For I was an hungred, and ye gave me meat: I was thirsty, and ye gave me drink: I was a stranger, and ye took me in:

Naked, and ye clothed me: I was sick, and ye visited me: I was in prison, and ye came unto me. . . .

And the King shall answer and say unto them, Verily I say unto you, Inasmuch as ye have done it unto one of the least of these my brethren, ye have done it unto me.
                    MATTHEW 25:34–36, 40

But when thou makest a feast, call the poor, the maimed, the lame, the blind:

And thou shalt be blessed; for they cannot recompense thee: for thou shalt be recompensed at the resurrection of the just.
                    LUKE 14:13–14

Well reported of for good works; if she have brought up children, if she have lodged strangers, if she have washed the saints' feet, if she have relieved the afflicted, if she have diligently followed every good work.   1 TIMOTHY 5:10

If a brother or sister be naked, and destitute of daily food,
     And one of you say unto them, Depart in peace, be ye warmed and filled; notwithstanding ye give them not those things which are needful to the body; what doth it profit?
                                                JAMES 2:15–16

For whosoever shall give you a cup of water to drink in my name, because ye belong to Christ, verily I say unto you, he shall not lose his reward.   MARK 9:41

Dear Lord,

I give my home to You.
Please fill it with love and laughter.
Help me to keep it in order,
so that I can be prepared to host
both friends and strangers.
Amen.

Humility

All of the charm and beauty
a woman may have amounts to nothing
if her ambitions are self-centered.
But if she reflects her Creator and assumes
the posture of a graceful servant,
she cannot help but command
high respect and love.

JEANNE HENDRICKS

Be not wise in your own conceits.   ROMANS 12:16

Thus saith the LORD, Let not the wise man glory in his wisdom, neither let the mighty man glory in his might, let not the rich man glory in his riches.   JEREMIAH 9:23

If I must needs glory, I will glory of the things which concern mine infirmities.   2 CORINTHIANS 11:30

The fear of the Lord is the instruction of wisdom; and before honour is humility.

PROVERBS 15:33

Boast not thyself of tomorrow; for thou knowest not what a day may bring forth.   PROVERBS 27:1

Whosoever therefore shall humble himself as this little child, the same is greatest in the kingdom of heaven.

MATTHEW 18:4

When men are cast down, then thou shalt say, There is lifting up; and he shall save the humble person.   JOB 22:29

Blessed are the poor in spirit: for theirs is the kingdom of heaven.   MATTHEW 5:3

Yea, all of you be subject one to another, and be clothed with humility: for God resisteth the proud, and giveth grace to the humble.

Humble yourselves therefore under the mighty hand of God, that he may exalt you in due time.   1 PETER 5:5–6

LORD, my heart is not haughty, nor mine eyes lofty: neither do I exercise myself in great matters, or in things too high for me.
PSALM 131:1

By humility and the fear of the LORD are riches, and honour, and life.   PROVERBS 22:4

Hearken to me, ye that follow after righteousness, ye that seek the LORD: look unto the rock whence ye are hewn, and to the hole of the pit whence ye are digged.   ISAIAH 51:1

LORD, thou hast heard the desire of the humble: thou wilt prepare their heart, thou wilt cause thine ear to hear.
PSALM 10:17

For thus saith the high and lofty One that inhabiteth eternity, whose name is Holy; I dwell in the high and holy place, with him also that is of a contrite and humble spirit, to revive the spirit of the humble, and to revive the heart of the contrite ones.   ISAIAH 57:15

Behold even to the moon, and it shineth not; yea, the stars are not pure in his sight.

How much less man, that is a worm? and the son of man, which is a worm?   JOB 25:5–6

But made himself of no reputation, and took upon him the form of a servant, and was made in the likeness of men:

And being found in fashion as a man, he humbled himself, and became obedient unto death, even the death of the cross.

Wherefore God also hath highly exalted him, and given him a name which is above every name.   PHILIPPIANS 2:7–9

Surely he scorneth the scorners: but he giveth grace unto the lowly.   PROVERBS 3:34

And whosoever shall exalt himself shall be abased; and he that shall humble himself shall be exalted.   MATTHEW 23:12

Though the LORD be high, yet hath he respect unto the lowly: but the proud he knoweth afar off.   PSALM 138:6

Humble yourselves in the sight of the Lord,
and he shall lift you up.

JAMES 4:10

When pride cometh, then cometh shame: but with the lowly is wisdom.   PROVERBS 11:2

When he maketh inquisition for blood, he remembereth them: he forgetteth not the cry of the humble.   PSALM 9:12

Better it is to be of an humble spirit with the lowly, than to divide the spoil with the proud.   PROVERBS 16:19

Dear Lord,

I often get caught in the performance trap.
I want so much to fit in, to earn acceptance,
to feel good about myself (and have others to do the same).
Help me to say "no" to the ego-builders
and "yes" to the humble.
Remind me that You don't look for performance.
You look for brokenness.
Then You create a miracle.
Amen.

Joy

L‍aughter lightens the load.

PATSY CLAIRMONT

And the angel said unto them, Fear not: for, behold, I bring you good tidings of great joy, which shall be to all people.

LUKE 2:10

The LORD is my strength and my shield; my heart trusted in him, and I am helped: therefore my heart greatly rejoiceth; and with my song will I praise him.   PSALM 28:7

Rejoice in the Lord alway: and again I say, Rejoice.

PHILIPPIANS 4:4

Hitherto have ye asked nothing in my name: ask, and ye shall receive, that your joy may be full.   JOHN 16:24

Be glad in the LORD, and rejoice, ye righteous: and shout for joy, all ye that are upright in heart.   PSALM 32:11

In the transgression of an evil man there is a snare: but the righteous doth sing and rejoice.   PROVERBS 29:6

As sorrowful, yet alway rejoicing; as poor, yet making many rich; as having nothing, and yet possessing all things.

2 CORINTHIANS 6:10

My lips shall greatly rejoice when I sing unto thee; and my soul, which thou hast redeemed.   PSALM 71:23

Therefore the redeemed of the LORD shall return, and come with singing unto Zion; and everlasting joy shall be upon their head: they shall obtain gladness and joy; and sorrow and mourning shall flee away.   ISAIAH 51:11

His lord said unto him, Well done, thou good and faithful servant: thou hast been faithful over a few things, I will make thee ruler over many things: enter thou into the joy of thy lord.

MATTHEW 25:21

Rejoice ye in that day, and leap for joy: for, behold, your reward is great in heaven: for in the like manner did their fathers unto the prophets.   LUKE 6:23

A merry heart doeth good
like a medicine.

PROVERBS 17:22

Make a joyful noise unto the LORD, all ye lands.
    Serve the LORD with gladness: come before his presence with singing.   PSALM 100:1–2

And now come I to thee; and these things I speak in the world, that they might have my joy fulfilled in themselves.

JOHN 17:13

All the days of the afflicted are evil: but he that is of a merry heart hath a continual feast.   PROVERBS 15:15

Is any merry? let him sing psalms.   JAMES 5:13

Let all those that seek thee rejoice and be glad in thee: let such as love thy salvation say continually, The LORD be magnified.

PSALM 40:16

And not only so, but we also joy in God through our Lord Jesus Christ, by whom we have now received the atonement.

ROMANS 5:11

Not for that we have dominion over your faith, but are helpers of your joy: for by faith ye stand.   2 CORINTHIANS 1:24

For our heart shall rejoice in him, because we have trusted in his holy name.   PSALM 33:21

Speaking to yourselves in psalms and hymns and spiritual songs, singing and making melody in your heart to the Lord.

EPHESIANS 5:19

I will greatly rejoice in the LORD, my soul shall be joyful in my God; for he hath clothed me with the garments of salvation, he hath covered me with the robe of righteousness, as a bridegroom decketh himself with ornaments, and as a bride adorneth herself with her jewels.   ISAIAH 61:10

LORD,

allow me see the humor in life.
Please don't let me take life too seriously.
Remind me to share my happiness with others—
my smile may be the only one another person receives today.
Amen.

Kindness

Let no one ever come to you
without leaving better and happier.
Be the living expression of God's kindness:
kindness in your face,
kindness in your eyes,
kindness in your smile.

MOTHER TERESA

Give to every man that asketh of thee; and of him that taketh away thy goods ask them not again.   LUKE 6:30

Not rendering evil for evil, or railing for railing: but contrariwise blessing; knowing that ye are thereunto called, that ye should inherit a blessing.   1 PETER 3:9

She openeth her mouth with wisdom; and in her tongue is the law of kindness.   PROVERBS 31:26

Put on therefore, as the elect of God, holy and beloved, bowels of mercies, kindness, humbleness of mind, meekness, longsuffering.   COLOSSIANS 3:12

And to godliness brotherly kindness; and to brotherly kindness charity.

For if these things be in you, and abound. . .ye shall neither be barren nor unfruitful in the knowledge of our Lord Jesus Christ.   2 PETER 1:7–8

The desire of a man is his kindness: and a poor man is better than a liar.

The fear of the LORD tendeth to life: and he that hath it shall abide satisfied.   PROVERBS 19:22–23

Thus speaketh the LORD of hosts, saying, Execute true judgment, and shew mercy and compassions every man to his brother:

And oppress not the widow, nor the fatherless, the stranger, nor the poor; and let none of you imagine evil against his brother in your heart.   ZECHARIAH 7:9–10

Let every one of us please his neighbour for his good to edification.   ROMANS 15:2

And if ye lend to them of whom ye hope to receive, what thank have ye? for sinners also lend to sinners, to receive as much again.

But love ye your enemies, and do good, and lend, hoping for nothing again; and your reward shall be great, and ye shall be the children of the Highest: for he is kind unto the unthankful and to the evil.   LUKE 6:34–35

He that despiseth
his neighbour sinneth:
but he that hath mercy on
the poor, happy is he.

PROVERBS 14:21

As we have therefore opportunity, let us do good unto all men, especially unto them who are of the household of faith.
                                                    GALATIANS 6:10

And he said, Blessed be thou of the LORD, my daughter: for thou hast shewed more kindness in the latter end than at the beginning. . . .

And now, my daughter, fear not; I will do to thee all that thou requirest.   RUTH 3:10–11

Rejoice with them that do rejoice, and weep with them that weep.

ROMANS 12:15

Give to him that asketh thee, and from him that would borrow of thee turn not thou away.

MATTHEW 5:42

Who can have compassion on the ignorant, and on them that are out of the way; for that he himself also is compassed with infirmity.

HEBREWS 5:2

But in all things approving ourselves as the ministers of God. . . .
By pureness, by knowledge, by longsuffering, by kindness. . .
as having nothing, and yet possessing all things.

2 CORINTHIANS 6:4, 6, 10

Heavenly Father,

please help me to be kind to those around me today.
Change my thoughts.
Control my tongue.
Let them see Your love through me.
Amen.

LOVE FOR OTHERS

If I put my own good name
before the other's highest good,
then I know nothing
of Calvary love.

AMY CARMICHAEL

Be kindly affectioned one to another with brotherly love; in honour preferring one another.   ROMANS 12:10

But as touching brotherly love ye need not that I write unto you: for ye yourselves are taught of God to love one another.
                    1 THESSALONIANS 4:9

For all the law is fulfilled in one word, even in this; Thou shalt love thy neighbour as thyself.   GALATIANS 5:14

And to godliness brotherly kindness; and to brotherly kindness charity.   2 PETER 1:7

Beloved, if God so loved us, we ought also to love one another.
    No man hath seen God at any time. If we love one another, God dwelleth in us, and his love is perfected in us.
                    1 JOHN 4:11–12

Thou shalt not avenge, nor bear any grudge against the children of thy people, but thou shalt love thy neighbour as thyself: I am the LORD.   LEVITICUS 19:18

Ye have heard that it hath been said, Thou shalt love thy neighbour, and hate thine enemy.
    But I say unto you, Love your enemies, bless them that curse you, do good to them that hate you, and pray for them which despitefully use you, and persecute you;
    That ye may be the children of your Father which is in heaven: for he maketh his sun to rise on the evil and on the good, and sendeth rain on the just and on the unjust.
                    MATTHEW 5:43–45

And now abideth faith, hope, charity, these three; but the greatest of these is charity.   1 CORINTHIANS 13:13

Owe no man any thing, but to love one another: for he that loveth another hath fulfilled the law.   ROMANS 13:8

For this is the message
that ye heard
from the beginning,
that we should love
one another.

1 JOHN 3:11

Though I speak with the tongues of men and of angels, and have not charity, I am become as sounding brass, or a tinkling cymbal.

And though I have the gift of prophecy, and understand all mysteries, and all knowledge; and though I have all faith, so that I could remove mountains, and have not charity, I am nothing.

And though I bestow all my goods to feed the poor, and though I give my body to be burned, and have not charity, it profiteth me nothing.   1 CORINTHIANS 13:1–3

And let us consider one another to provoke unto love and to good works.   HEBREWS 10:24

In this the children of God are manifest, and the children of the devil: whosoever doeth not righteousness is not of God, neither he that loveth not his brother. 1 JOHN 3:10

And through thy knowledge shall the weak brother perish, for whom Christ died?

But when ye sin so against the brethren, and wound their weak conscience, ye sin against Christ.

1 CORINTHIANS 8:11–12

He that loveth not knoweth not God; for God is love.

1 JOHN 4:8

This is my commandment, That ye love one another, as I have loved you.

Greater love hath no man than this, that a man lay down his life for his friends. JOHN 15:12–13

I speak to your shame. Is it so, that there is not a wise man among you? no, not one that shall be able to judge between his brethren?

But brother goeth to law with brother, and that before the unbelievers.

Now therefore there is utterly a fault among you, because ye go to law one with another. Why do ye not rather take wrong? why do ye not rather suffer yourselves to be defrauded?

Nay, ye do wrong, and defraud, and that your brethren.

1 CORINTHIANS 6:5–8

Honour all men. Love the brotherhood. Fear God. Honour the king. 1 PETER 2:17

Leave there thy gift before the altar, and go thy way; first be reconciled to thy brother, and then come and offer thy gift.

MATTHEW 5:24

If a man say, I love God, and hateth his brother, he is a liar: for he that loveth not his brother whom he hath seen, how can he love God whom he hath not seen?

And this commandment have we from him, That he who loveth God love his brother also.   1 JOHN 4:20–21

And this I pray,
that your love may abound
yet more and more in
knowledge and in all judgment.

PHILIPPIANS 1:9

Hereby perceive we the love of God, because he laid down his life for us: and we ought to lay down our lives for the brethren.

But whoso hath this world's good, and seeth his brother have need, and shutteth up his bowels of compassion from him, how dwelleth the love of God in him?

My little children, let us not love in word, neither in tongue; but in deed and in truth.

And hereby we know that we are of the truth, and shall assure our hearts before him.   1 JOHN 3:16–19

Seeing ye have purified your souls in obeying the truth through the Spirit unto unfeigned love of the brethren, see that ye love one another with a pure heart fervently.   1 PETER 1:22

For, brethren, ye have been called unto liberty; only use not liberty for an occasion to the flesh, but by love serve one another.

For all the law is fulfilled in one word, even in this; Thou shalt love thy neighbour as thyself.   GALATIANS 5:13–14

A new commandment I give unto you, That ye love one another; as I have loved you, that ye also love one another.

By this shall all men know that ye are my disciples, if ye have love one to another.   JOHN 13:34–35

Beloved, let us love one another: for love is of God; and every one that loveth is born of God, and knoweth God.

He that loveth not knoweth not God; for God is love.

In this was manifested the love of God toward us, because that God sent his only begotten Son into the world, that we might live through him.

Herein is love, not that we loved God, but that he loved us, and sent his Son to be the propitiation for our sins.

Beloved, if God so loved us, we ought also to love one another.   1 JOHN 4:7–11

Finally, be ye all of one mind, having compassion one of another, love as brethren, be pitiful, be courteous.   1 PETER 3:8

Heavenly Father,

help me to love others unconditionally.
As I'm reminded that You love me
in spite of my imperfections,
let me extend that same love to those
I come in contact with.
Amen.

Meekness

We can do no great things;
only small things
with great love.

MOTHER TERESA

Good and upright is the LORD: therefore will he teach sinners in the way.

The meek will he guide in judgment: and the meek will he teach his way.   PSALM 25:8–9

Great is our Lord, and of great power: his understanding is infinite.

The Lord lifteth up the meek: he casteth the wicked down to the ground.   PSALM 147:5–6

But the meek shall
inherit the earth;
and shall delight themselves
in the abundance of peace.

PSALM 37:11

Likewise, ye wives, be in subjection to your own husbands; that if any obey not the word, they also may without the word be won by the conversation of the wives. . . .

Whose adorning let it not be that outward adorning of plaiting the hair, and of wearing of gold, or of putting on of apparel;

But let it be the hidden man of the heart, in that which is not corruptible, even the ornament of a meek and quiet spirit, which is in the sight of God of great price.   1 PETER 3:1, 3–4

The meek shall eat and be satisfied: they shall praise the LORD that seek him: your heart shall live for ever.   PSALM 22:26

The meek also shall increase their joy in the LORD, and the poor among men shall rejoice in the Holy One of Israel.

ISAIAH 29:19

Seek ye the LORD, all ye meek of the earth, which have wrought his judgment; seek righteousness, seek meekness: it may be ye shall be hid in the day of the LORD'S anger.   ZEPHANIAH 2:3

The Spirit of the Lord God is upon me; because the LORD hath anointed me to preach good tidings unto the meek; he hath sent me to bind up the brokenhearted, to proclaim liberty to the captives, and the opening of the prison to them that are bound.

ISAIAH 61:1

Blessed are the meek: for they shall inherit the earth.

MATTHEW 5:5

Brethren, if a man be overtaken in a fault, ye which are spiritual, restore such an one in the spirit of meekness; considering thyself, lest thou also be tempted.

Bear ye one another's burdens, and so fulfil the law of Christ.   GALATIANS 6:1–2

For the LORD taketh pleasure in his people: he will beautify the meek with salvation.   PSALM 149:4

Lord God,

I pray that I will have a spirit of meekness.
Help me to follow Your example,
being mild, yet not weak.
For if I can maintain this balance,
I will have strength through You.
Amen.

Mercy

God deals with us
from a merciful posture;
His arms are open,
His words are healing,
He wants sinners to
return to Him.

MARTIE STOWELL

Be ye therefore merciful, as your Father also is merciful.

LUKE 6:36

But thou, O Lord, art a God full of compassion, and gracious, longsuffering, and plenteous in mercy and truth.

PSALM 86:15

Therefore turn thou to thy God: keep mercy and judgment, and wait on thy God continually.   HOSEA 12:6

He that covereth his sins
shall not prosper:
but whoso confesseth
and forsaketh them
shall have mercy.

PROVERBS 28:13

He hath shewed thee, O man, what is good; and what doth the LORD require of thee, but to do justly, and to love mercy, and to walk humbly with thy God?   MICAH 6:8

Behold, we count them happy which endure. Ye have heard of the patience of Job, and have seen the end of the Lord; that the Lord is very pitiful, and of tender mercy.   JAMES 5:11

Blessed are the merciful: for they shall obtain mercy.

MATTHEW 5:7

For thou, Lord, art good, and ready to forgive; and plenteous in mercy unto all them that call upon thee.   PSALM 86:5

Blessed be the God and Father of our Lord Jesus Christ, which according to his abundant mercy hath begotten us again unto a lively hope by the resurrection of Jesus Christ from the dead.

1 PETER 1:3

Thou art a God ready to pardon, gracious and merciful, slow to anger, and of great kindness.   NEHEMIAH 9:17

But God, who is rich in mercy, for his great love wherewith he loved us,

Even when we were dead in sins, hath quickened us together with Christ, (by grace ye are saved).   EPHESIANS 2:4–5

Not by works of righteousness which we have done, but according to his mercy he saved us, by the washing of regeneration, and renewing of the Holy Ghost;

Which he shed on us abundantly through Jesus Christ our Saviour;

That being justified by his grace, we should be made heirs according to the hope of eternal life.   TITUS 3:5–7

Let not mercy and truth forsake thee: bind them about thy neck; write them upon the table of thine heart:

So shalt thou find favour and good understanding in the sight of God and man.   PROVERBS 3:3–4

For I will be merciful to their unrighteousness, and their sins and their iniquities will I remember no more.

In that he saith, A new covenant, he hath made the first old. Now that which decayeth and waxeth old is ready to vanish away.   HEBREWS 8:12–13

For God hath concluded them all in unbelief, that he might have mercy upon all.   ROMANS 11:32

The LORD is good to all: and his tender mercies are over all his works.   PSALM 145:9

Let the wicked forsake his way, and the unrighteous man his thoughts: and let him return unto the LORD, and he will have mercy upon him; and to our God, for he will abundantly pardon.
                                    ISAIAH 55:7

And his mercy is on them that fear him from generation to generation.   LUKE 1:50

Mercy and truth are met together; righteousness and peace have kissed each other.   PSALM 85:10

Father,
forgive me for keeping record of wrongs
others have committed against me.
Just as You have forgotten all of my sins and failures,
let me show that same mercy to others.
Erase the wrongs from my memory, I pray.
Amen.

Modesty

A woman with a gentle and quiet spirit
is not only precious to God,
but she is attractive to others also.
She dresses appropriately,
but it is her inner adornment that is
noted because she is secure
and at rest within her spirit.

CYNTHIA HEALD

In like manner also, that women adorn themselves in modest apparel, with shamefacedness and sobriety; not with braided hair, or gold, or pearls, or costly array;

But (which becometh women professing godliness) with good works.   1 TIMOTHY 2:9–10

A man's pride shall
bring him low:
but honour shall
uphold the humble in spirit.

PROVERBS 29:23

The aged women likewise, that they be in behaviour as becometh holiness, not false accusers, not given to much wine, teachers of good things;

That they may teach the young women to be sober, to love their husbands, to love their children,

To be discreet, chaste, keepers at home, good, obedient to their own husbands, that the word of God be not blasphemed.
                                                       TITUS 2:3–5

Let no man deceive himself. If any man among you seemeth to be wise in this world, let him become a fool, that he may be wise.   1 CORINTHIANS 3:18

But now ye rejoice in your boastings: all such rejoicing is evil.

JAMES 4:16

Let another man praise thee, and not thine own mouth; a stranger, and not thine own lips.   PROVERBS 27:2

And base things of the world, and things which are despised, hath God chosen, yea, and things which are not, to bring to nought things that are:

That no flesh should glory in his presence.

1 CORINTHIANS 1:28–29

Dear Lord,

I want to demonstrate modesty in my life.
I will clothe myself outwardly
in a manner that pleases You
and will adorn myself inwardly with a gentle spirit.
Amen.

Obedience

The only way I will keep
a pliable, obedient spirit
in the larger decisions
is to look to Him and to obey
in the smaller ones.

CATHERINE MARSHALL

Now therefore, if ye will obey my voice indeed, and keep my covenant, then ye shall be a peculiar treasure unto me above all people: for all the earth is mine.   EXODUS 19:5

Thou shalt keep therefore his statutes, and his commandments, which I command thee this day, that it may go well with thee, and with thy children after thee, and that thou mayest prolong thy days upon the earth, which the LORD thy God giveth thee, for ever.   DEUTERONOMY 4:40

Observe and hear all these words which I command thee, that it may go well with thee, and with thy children after thee for ever, when thou doest that which is good and right in the sight of the LORD thy God.   DEUTERONOMY 12:28

My son, forget not my law; but let thine heart keep my commandments:
    For length of days, and long life, and peace, shall they add to thee.   PROVERBS 3:1–2

But whoso looketh into the perfect law of liberty, and continueth therein, he being not a forgetful hearer, but a doer of the work, this man shall be blessed in his deed.   JAMES 1:25

Those things, which ye have both learned, and received, and heard, and seen in me, do: and the God of peace shall be with you.   PHILIPPIANS 4:9

Not every one that saith unto me, Lord, Lord, shall enter into the kingdom of heaven; but he that doeth the will of my Father which is in heaven.   MATTHEW 7:21

I command thee this day to love the LORD thy God, to walk in his ways, and to keep his commandments and his statutes and his judgments, that thou mayest live and multiply: and the LORD thy God shall bless thee in the land whither thou goest to possess it. DEUTERONOMY 30:16

If they obey and serve him,
they shall spend their days in prosperity,
and their years
in pleasures.

JOB 36:11

Let us hear the conclusion of the whole matter: Fear God, and keep his commandments: for this is the whole duty of man.
ECCLESIASTES 12:13

If ye keep my commandments, ye shall abide in my love; even as I have kept my Father's commandments, and abide in his love. JOHN 15:10

Whosoever therefore shall break one of these least commandments, and shall teach men so, he shall be called the least in the kingdom of heaven: but whosoever shall do and teach them, the same shall be called great in the kingdom of heaven.
MATTHEW 5:19

All the paths of the LORD are mercy and truth unto such as keep his covenant and his testimonies.   PSALM 25:10

And Samuel said, Hath the LORD as great delight in burnt offerings and sacrifices, as in obeying the voice of the LORD? Behold, to obey is better than sacrifice, and to hearken than the fat of rams.   1 SAMUEL 15:22

For not the hearers of the law are just before God, but the doers of the law shall be justified.   ROMANS 2:13

And the world passeth away, and the lust thereof: but he that doeth the will of God abideth for ever.   1 JOHN 2:17

But he said, Yea rather, blessed are they that hear the word of God, and keep it.   LUKE 11:28

Keep therefore the words of this covenant, and do them, that ye may prosper in all that ye do.   DEUTERONOMY 29:9

Furthermore we have had fathers of our flesh which corrected us, and we gave them reverence: shall we not much rather be in subjection unto the Father of spirits, and live?   HEBREWS 12:9

Blessed are they that keep his testimonies, and that seek him with the whole heart.   PSALM 119:2

Wherefore, my beloved, as ye have always obeyed, not as in my presence only, but now much more in my absence, work out your own salvation with fear and trembling.

                                    PHILIPPIANS 2:12

If ye be willing and obedient, ye shall eat the good of the land.
ISAIAH 1:19

Father,
the path of life is often difficult.
I ask not that You make it smooth,
but to illuminate it so that I can see to walk in obedience.
If for a moment the light is dim,
let me walk by faith, trusting You with each step I take.
For Your way is perfect. Amen.

Patience

Obedience is the fruit of faith;
patience, the bloom
on the fruit.

CHRISTINA ROSSETTI

And the servant of the Lord must not strive; but be gentle unto all men, apt to teach, patient.   2 TIMOTHY 2:24

Rest in the LORD, and wait patiently for him: fret not thyself because of him who prospereth in his way, because of the man who bringeth wicked devices to pass.

Cease from anger, and forsake wrath: fret not thyself in any wise to do evil.

For evildoers shall be cut off: but those that wait upon the LORD, they shall inherit the earth.   PSALM 37:7–9

For ye have need of patience, that,
after ye have done the will of God,
ye might receive the promise.

HEBREWS 10:36

For whatsoever things were written aforetime were written for our learning, that we through patience and comfort of the scriptures might have hope.

Now the God of patience and consolation grant you to be likeminded one toward another according to Christ Jesus.   ROMANS 15:4–5

And let us not be weary in well doing: for in due season we shall reap, if we faint not.   GALATIANS 6:9

Knowing this, that the trying of your faith worketh patience.

But let patience have her perfect work, that ye may be perfect and entire, wanting nothing.   JAMES 1:3–4

But that on the good ground are they, which in an honest and good heart, having heard the word, keep it, and bring forth fruit with patience.   LUKE 8:15

And not only so, but we glory in tribulations also: knowing that tribulation worketh patience;

And patience, experience; and experience, hope.
                                                        ROMANS 5:3–4

But in all things approving ourselves as the ministers of God, in much patience, in afflictions, in necessities, in distresses.
                                                      2 CORINTHIANS 6:4

In your patience possess ye your souls.   LUKE 21:19

That ye be not slothful, but followers of them who through faith and patience inherit the promises.   HEBREWS 6:12

And so, after he had patiently endured, he obtained the promise.   HEBREWS 6:15

Be patient therefore, brethren, unto the coming of the Lord. Behold, the husbandman waiteth for the precious fruit of the earth, and hath long patience for it, until he receive the early and latter rain.

Be ye also patient; stablish your hearts: for the coming of the Lord draweth nigh.   JAMES 5:7–8

Now we exhort you, brethren, warn them that are unruly, comfort the feebleminded, support the weak, be patient toward all men.   1 THESSALONIANS 5:14

Wherefore seeing we also are compassed about with so great a cloud of witnesses, let us lay aside every weight, and the sin which doth so easily beset us, and let us run with patience the race that is set before us.   HEBREWS 12:1

To them who by patient continuance
in well doing seek for glory and honour
and immortality, eternal life.

ROMANS 2:7

For what glory is it, if, when ye be buffeted for your faults, ye shall take it patiently? but if, when ye do well, and suffer for it, ye take it patiently, this is acceptable with God.
                    1 PETER 2:20

Better is the end of a thing than the beginning thereof: and the patient in spirit is better than the proud in spirit.

Be not hasty in thy spirit to be angry: for anger resteth in the bosom of fools.   ECCLESIASTES 7:8–9

And the Lord direct your hearts into the love of God, and into the patient waiting for Christ. 2 THESSALONIANS 3:5

Lord,

sometimes I look for a sign.
I want the writing on the wall or a burning bush experience.
I feel like I need direction, and I need it now!
Lord, give me patience. Give me faith.
Instead of seeking a sign,
let me live expectantly for the everyday miracles
and listen for Your still, small voice.

Peace

When the presence
of the Lord
really becomes your
experience, you will
actually discover that
you have gradually begun to love this silence
and peaceful rest which come with
His presence.

MADAME GUYON

For the mountains shall depart, and the hills be removed; but my kindness shall not depart from thee, neither shall the covenant of my peace be removed, saith the Lord that hath mercy on thee.

And all thy children shall be taught of the LORD; and great shall be the peace of thy children.   ISAIAH 54:10, 13

Now the God of hope fill you with all joy and peace in believing, that ye may abound in hope, through the power of the Holy Ghost.   ROMANS 15:13

The LORD will give strength unto his people; the LORD will bless his people with peace.   PSALM 29:11

When a man's ways please the LORD, he maketh even his enemies to be at peace with him.   PROVERBS 16:7

Blessed are the peacemakers: for they shall be called the children of God.   MATTHEW 5:9

Deceit is in the heart of them that imagine evil: but to the counsellors of peace is joy.   PROVERBS 12:20

And the fruit of righteousness is sown in peace of them that make peace.   JAMES 3:18

Endeavouring to keep the unity of the Spirit in the bond of peace.   EPHESIANS 4:3

Glory to God in the highest, and on earth peace, good will toward men.   LUKE 2:14

Flee also youthful lusts: but follow righteousness, faith, charity, peace, with them that call on the Lord out of a pure heart.

2 TIMOTHY 2:22

Mark the perfect man, and behold the upright: for the end of that man is peace.   PSALM 37:37

If it be possible, as much as lieth in you, live peaceably with all men.   ROMANS 12:18

Thou wilt keep him
in perfect peace,
whose mind is stayed on thee:
because he trusteth in thee.

ISAIAH 26:3

And he shall judge among the nations, and shall rebuke many people: and they shall beat their swords into plowshares, and their spears into pruninghooks: nation shall not lift up sword against nation, neither shall they learn war any more.   ISAIAH 2:4

For he that will love life, and see good days, let him refrain his tongue from evil, and his lips that they speak no guile:

Let him eschew evil, and do good; let him seek peace, and ensue it.   1 PETER 3:10–11

And the peace of God, which passeth all understanding, shall keep your hearts and minds through Christ Jesus.

PHILIPPIANS 4:7

And to esteem them very highly in love for their work's sake. And be at peace among yourselves.   1 THESSALONIANS 5:13

I exhort therefore, that, first of all, supplications, prayers, intercessions, and giving of thanks, be made for all men;

For kings, and for all that are in authority; that we may lead a quiet and peaceable life in all godliness and honesty.

1 TIMOTHY 2:1–2

Follow peace with all men, and holiness, without which no man shall see the Lord.   HEBREWS 12:14

Behold, how good and how pleasant it is for brethren to dwell together in unity!   PSALM 133:1

For God hath not given us the spirit of fear; but of power, and of love, and of a sound mind.   2 TIMOTHY 1:7

Peace I leave with you, my peace I give unto you: not as the world giveth, give I unto you. Let not your heart be troubled, neither let it be afraid.   JOHN 14:27

LORD,
I often become distracted with the activities of everyday life.
Please give me a calm spirit,
and help me to rest in Your perfect peace. Amen.

Perseverance

You may have to fight a battle
more than once to win it.

MARGARET THATCHER

For the which cause I also suffer these things: nevertheless I am not ashamed: for I know whom I have believed, and am persuaded that he is able to keep that which I have committed unto him against that day.

Hold fast the form of sound words, which thou hast heard of me, in faith and love which is in Christ Jesus.

2 TIMOTHY 1:12–13

He that hath an ear, let him hear what the Spirit saith unto the churches; He that overcometh shall not be hurt of the second death.

REVELATION 2:11

For we are made partakers of Christ, if we hold the beginning of our confidence stedfast unto the end.

HEBREWS 3:14

To him that overcometh will I grant to sit with me in my throne, even as I also overcame, and am set down with my Father in his throne.

REVELATION 3:21

That the trial of your faith, being much more precious than of gold that perisheth, though it be tried with fire, might be found unto praise and honour and glory at the appearing of Jesus Christ.

1 PETER 1:7

Praying always with all prayer and supplication in the Spirit, and watching thereunto with all perseverance and supplication for all saints.

EPHESIANS 6:18

Stand fast therefore in the liberty wherewith Christ hath made us free, and be not entangled again with the yoke of bondage.

GALATIANS 5:1

Teaching us that, denying ungodliness and worldly lusts, we should live soberly, righteously, and godly, in this present world;

Looking for that blessed hope, and the glorious appearing of the great God and our Saviour Jesus Christ.

TITUS 2:12–13

Though he fall, he shall not be utterly cast down: for the LORD upholdeth him with his hand.   PSALM 37:24

*T*hou therefore endure
hardness, as a good soldier
of Jesus Christ.

2 TIMOTHY 2:3

Let us hold fast the profession of our faith without wavering; (for he is faithful that promised).   HEBREWS 10:23

Wherefore seeing we also are compassed about with so great a cloud of witnesses, let us lay aside every weight, and the sin which doth so easily beset us, and let us run with patience the race that is set before us,

Looking unto Jesus the author and finisher of our faith; who for the joy that was set before him endured the cross, despising the shame, and is set down at the right hand of the throne of God.   HEBREWS 12:1–2

For I am persuaded, that neither death, nor life, nor angels, nor principalities, nor powers, nor things present, nor things to come, Nor height, nor depth, nor any other creature, shall be able to separate us from the love of God, which is in Christ Jesus our Lord.   ROMANS 8:38–39

But the path of the just is as the shining light, that shineth more and more unto the perfect day.   PROVERBS 4:18

Then said Jesus to those Jews which believed on him, If ye continue in my word, then are ye my disciples indeed.

JOHN 8:31

Ye therefore, beloved, seeing ye know these things before, beware lest ye also, being led away with the error of the wicked, fall from your own stedfastness.   2 PETER 3:17

For now we live, if ye stand fast in the Lord.

1 THESSALONIANS 3:8

Confirming the souls of the disciples, and exhorting them to continue in the faith, and that we must through much tribulation enter into the kingdom of God.   ACTS 14:22

Who shall separate us from the love of Christ? shall tribulation, or distress, or persecution, or famine, or nakedness, or peril, or sword?   ROMANS 8:35

Wherefore take unto you the whole armour of God, that ye may be able to withstand in the evil day, and having done all, to stand.   EPHESIANS 6:13

Therefore, my brethren dearly beloved and longed for, my joy
and crown, so stand fast in the Lord, my dearly beloved.

PHILIPPIANS 4:1

Father,

sometimes I get so weary and want to give up.
But You have promised a life of blessing if I will persevere.
Thank You for giving me the strength I need to "run the race."
Amen.

Power

The stone still stood there
in that quiet garden,
a reminder of the reality
of the problem we all must live with;
but Christ had moved it
to one side so very easily,
demonstrating his resurrection power
on our behalf.

JILL BRISCOE

Seek the LORD and his strength, seek his face continually.

1 CHRONICLES 16:11

The LORD thy God in the midst of thee is mighty; he will save, he will rejoice over thee with joy; he will rest in his love, he will joy over thee with singing.   ZEPHANIAH 3:17

Now unto him that is able to do exceeding abundantly above all that we ask or think, according to the power that worketh in us.   EPHESIANS 3:20

For the kingdom of God
is not in word,
but in power.

1 CORINTHIANS 4:20

But ye shall receive power, after that the Holy Ghost is come upon you: and ye shall be witnesses unto me both in Jerusalem, and in all Judaea, and in Samaria, and unto the uttermost part of the earth.   ACTS 1:8

For our gospel came not unto you in word only, but also in power, and in the Holy Ghost, and in much assurance; as ye know what manner of men we were among you for your sake.

1 THESSALONIANS 1:5

And what is the exceeding greatness of his power to us-ward who believe, according to the working of his mighty power,

Which he wrought in Christ, when he raised him from the dead, and set him at his own right hand in the heavenly places.

EPHESIANS 1:19–20

For though he was crucified through weakness, yet he liveth by the power of God. For we also are weak in him, but we shall live with him by the power of God toward you.

2 CORINTHIANS 13:4

O Lord,

I know Your power is great. . .
greater than any other source on earth.
Remind me when I feel weak today
that Your strength is sufficient.
Amen.

Prayer

Prayer is an indispensable part
of our relationship
with Jesus Christ.

LAUREL OKE LOGAN

And in that day ye shall ask me nothing. Verily, verily, I say unto you, Whatsoever ye shall ask the Father in my name, he will give it you.

Hitherto have ye asked nothing in my name: ask, and ye shall receive, that your joy may be full.   JOHN 16:23–24

But thou, when thou prayest, enter into thy closet, and when thou hast shut thy door, pray to thy Father which is in secret; and thy Father which seeth in secret shall reward thee openly.

But when ye pray, use not vain repetitions, as the heathen do: for they think that they shall be heard for their much speaking.
                                                      MATTHEW 6:6–7

Give ear to my words, O LORD, consider my meditation.

Hearken unto the voice of my cry, my King, and my God: for unto thee will I pray.

My voice shalt thou hear in the morning, O LORD; in the morning will I direct my prayer unto thee, and will look up.
                                                      PSALM 5:1–3

But we will give ourselves continually to prayer, and to the ministry of the word.   ACTS 6:4

If ye then, being evil, know how to give good gifts unto your children, how much more shall your Father which is in heaven give good things to them that ask him?   MATTHEW 7:11

Rejoicing in hope; patient in tribulation; continuing instant in prayer.   ROMANS 12:12

Pray without ceasing.   1 THESSALONIANS 5:17

Evening, and morning, and at noon, will I pray, and cry aloud:
and he shall hear my voice.   PSALM 55:17

He will be very gracious unto thee at the voice of thy cry; when
he shall hear it, he will answer thee.   ISAIAH 30:19

Thou shalt make thy prayer unto him, and he shall hear thee,
and thou shalt pay thy vows.   JOB 22:27

And all things, whatsoever
ye shall ask in prayer,
believing, ye shall receive.

MATTHEW 21:22

Praying always with all prayer and supplication in the Spirit,
and watching thereunto with all perseverance and supplication
for all saints.   EPHESIANS 6:18

I waited patiently for the LORD; and he inclined unto me, and
heard my cry.   PSALM 40:1

Then shall ye call upon me, and ye shall go and pray unto me,
and I will hearken unto you.
    And ye shall seek me, and find me, when ye shall search for
me with all your heart.   JEREMIAH 29:12–13

And shall not God avenge his own elect, which cry day and night unto him, though he bear long with them?   LUKE 18:7

If my people, which are called by my name, shall humble themselves, and pray, and seek my face, and turn from their wicked ways; then will I hear from heaven, and will forgive their sin, and will heal their land.   2 CHRONICLES 7:14

The LORD is nigh unto all them that call upon him, to all that call upon him in truth.   PSALM 145:18

Let us therefore come boldly unto the throne of grace, that we may obtain mercy, and find grace to help in time of need.   HEBREWS 4:16

The sacrifice of the wicked is an abomination to the LORD: but the prayer of the upright is his delight.   PROVERBS 15:8

Ask, and it shall be given you; seek, and ye shall find; knock, and it shall be opened unto you:
For every one that asketh receiveth; and he that seeketh findeth; and to him that knocketh it shall be opened.   MATTHEW 7:7–8

And it shall come to pass, that before they call, I will answer; and while they are yet speaking, I will hear.   ISAIAH 65:24

Likewise the Spirit also helpeth our infirmities: for we know not what we should pray for as we ought: but the Spirit itself maketh intercession for us with groanings which cannot be uttered.   ROMANS 8:26

Confess your faults one to another, and pray one for another, that ye may be healed. The effectual fervent prayer of a righteous man availeth much.   JAMES 5:16

And this is the confidence that we have in him, that, if we ask any thing according to his will, he heareth us:

And if we know that he hear us, whatsoever we ask, we know that we have the petitions that we desired of him.
                                                    1 JOHN 5:14–15

I will therefore that men pray every where,
lifting up holy hands,
without wrath and doubting.

1 TIMOTHY 2:8

Oh that men would praise the LORD for his goodness, and for his wonderful works to the children of men!   PSALM 107:15

I will pray with the spirit, and I will pray with the understanding also: I will sing with the spirit, and I will sing with the understanding also.   1 CORINTHIANS 14:15

Yet the LORD will command his lovingkindness in the daytime, and in the night his song shall be with me, and my prayer unto the God of my life.   PSALM 42:8

Again I say unto you, That if two of you shall agree on earth as touching any thing that they shall ask, it shall be done for them of my Father which is in heaven.

For where two or three are gathered together in my name, there am I in the midst of them.   MATTHEW 18:19–20

So that they cause the cry of the poor to come unto him, and he heareth the cry of the afflicted.   JOB 34:28

He shall call upon me, and I will answer him.   PSALM 91:15

Because he hath inclined his ear unto me, therefore will I call upon him as long as I live.   PSALM 116:2

Is any among you afflicted? let him pray. Is any merry? let him sing psalms.

Is any sick among you? let him call for the elders of the church; and let them pray over him, anointing him with oil in the name of the Lord:

And the prayer of faith shall save the sick, and the Lord shall raise him up; and if he have committed sins, they shall be forgiven him.   JAMES 5:13–15

Be careful for nothing; but in every thing by prayer and supplication with thanksgiving let your requests be made known unto God.

And the peace of God, which passeth all understanding, shall keep your hearts and minds through Christ Jesus.

PHILIPPIANS 4:6–7

Dear God,

I pray for my friends and family.
Please protect them and help them to grow closer to You each day.
I pray this for myself, also, Lord.
I want to communicate with You continually,
sharing from my heart, then
quietly and patiently waiting for Your voice.
Thank You, Father, for listening to my prayer.
Amen.

Pride

Why are we not
far more frightened
of what pride can do?
Pride can cost us—
and probably those after us.

BETH MOORE

Be not wise in thine own eyes: fear the LORD, and depart from evil.   PROVERBS 3:7

And he sat down, and called the twelve, and saith unto them, If any man desire to be first, the same shall be last of all, and servant of all.   MARK 9:35

Surely God will not hear vanity, neither will the Almighty regard it.   JOB 35:13

P ride goeth before
destruction, and an haughty spirit before a fall.

PROVERBS 16:18

An high look, and a proud heart, and the plowing of the wicked, is sin.   PROVERBS 21:4

Be of the same mind one toward another. Mind not high things, but condescend to men of low estate. Be not wise in your own conceits.   ROMANS 12:16

And he said unto them, Ye are they which justify yourselves before men; but God knoweth your hearts: for that which is highly esteemed among men is abomination in the sight of God.

LUKE 16:15

But now ye rejoice in your boastings: all such rejoicing is evil.
JAMES 4:16

Talk no more so exceeding proudly; let not arrogancy come out of your mouth: for the LORD is a God of knowledge, and by him actions are weighed.   1 SAMUEL 2:3

The fear of the LORD is to hate evil: pride, and arrogancy, and the evil way, and the froward mouth, do I hate.
PROVERBS 8:13

Let not the foot of pride come against me, and let not the hand of the wicked remove me.   PSALM 36:11

He that is of a proud heart stirreth up strife: but he that putteth his trust in the LORD shall be made fat.

He that trusteth in his own heart is a fool: but whoso walketh wisely, he shall be delivered.   PROVERBS 28:25–26

Woe unto them that are wise in their own eyes, and prudent in their own sight!   ISAIAH 5:21

But he that glorieth, let him glory in the Lord.

For not he that commendeth himself is approved, but whom the Lord commendeth.   2 CORINTHIANS 10:17–18

How can ye believe, which receive honour one of another, and seek not the honour that cometh from God only?   JOHN 5:44

When pride cometh, then cometh shame: but with the lowly is wisdom.   PROVERBS 11:2

For I say, through the grace given unto me, to every man that is among you, not to think of himself more highly than he ought to think; but to think soberly, according as God hath dealt to every man the measure of faith.   ROMANS 12:3

For if a man think himself to be something, when he is nothing, he deceiveth himself.   GALATIANS 6:3

Heavenly Father,

forgive me for my pride.
I am no better than anyone,
and You consider Your children as equals.
I am humbled, Lord,
that You have adopted me into Your family
and call me Your friend. Amen.

PROTECTION

G od will never lead you
where His strength
cannot keep you.

BARBARA JOHNSON

The LORD of hosts is with us; the God of Jacob is our refuge. Selah.   PSALM 46:7

In the fear of the LORD is strong confidence: and his children shall have a place of refuge.   PROVERBS 14:26

When thou passest through the waters, I will be with thee; and through the rivers, they shall not overflow thee: when thou walkest through the fire, thou shalt not be burned; neither shall the flame kindle upon thee.   ISAIAH 43:2

The name of the LORD
is a strong tower:
the righteous runneth into it, and is safe.

PROVERBS 18:10

But the LORD is my defence; and my God is the rock of my refuge.   PSALM 94:22

Be thou my strong habitation, whereunto I may continually resort: thou hast given commandment to save me, for thou art my rock and my fortress.   PSALM 71:3

Above all, taking the shield of faith, wherewith ye shall be able to quench all the fiery darts of the wicked.   EPHESIANS 6:16

For thou, LORD, wilt bless the righteous; with favour wilt thou compass him as with a shield.   PSALM 5:12

The LORD liveth; and blessed be my rock; and exalted be the God of the rock of my salvation.   2 SAMUEL 22:47

Thou hast also given me the shield of thy salvation: and thy right hand hath holden me up, and thy gentleness hath made me great.   PSALM 18:35

Our soul waiteth for the LORD: he is our help and our shield.
                    PSALM 33:20

Every word of God is pure: he is a shield unto them that put their trust in him.   PROVERBS 30:5

He shall cover thee with his feathers, and under his wings shalt thou trust: his truth shall be thy shield and buckler.
                    PSALM 91:4

The LORD is my rock, and my fortress, and my deliverer; my God, my strength, in whom I will trust; my buckler, and the horn of my salvation, and my high tower.   PSALM 18:2

And he said, The LORD is my rock, and my fortress, and my deliverer;

The God of my rock; in him will I trust: he is my shield, and the horn of my salvation, my high tower, and my refuge, my saviour; thou savest me from violence.

I will call on the LORD, who is worthy to be praised: so shall I be saved from mine enemies.   2 SAMUEL 22:2–4

But whoso hearkeneth unto me shall dwell safely, and shall be quiet from fear of evil.   PROVERBS 1:33

The Lord is good,
a strong hold in the day of trouble;
and he knoweth them that trust in him.

NAHUM 1:7

Cast thy burden upon the LORD, and he shall sustain thee: he shall never suffer the righteous to be moved.   PSALM 55:22

For thou art my rock and my fortress; therefore for thy name's sake lead me, and guide me.   PSALM 31:3

God is our refuge and strength, a very present help in trouble.
     Therefore will not we fear, though the earth be removed, and though the mountains be carried into the midst of the sea;
     Though the waters thereof roar and be troubled, though the mountains shake with the swelling thereof. Selah.
                                                        PSALM 46:1–3

The eternal God is thy refuge, and underneath are the everlasting arms.   DEUTERONOMY 33:27

The LORD also will be a refuge for the oppressed, a refuge in times of trouble.   PSALM 9:9

God is our refuge and strength, a very present help in trouble.
                                                    PSALM 46:1

Dear Father,

thank You for Your physical protection
as well as spiritual protection.
There are so many occasions when I could falter,
but You guard my feet. I trust You to protect me today.
Amen.

Purity

A person of purity
stands before his peers
and superiors
and courageously maintains
his faith in God.

CINDY TRENT

Drink waters out of thine own cistern, and running waters out of thine own well.   PROVERBS 5:15

Mortify therefore your members which are upon the earth; fornication, uncleanness, inordinate affection, evil concupiscence, and covetousness, which is idolatry:

For which things' sake the wrath of God cometh on the children of disobedience.   COLOSSIANS 3:5–6

Thou shalt not commit adultery.   EXODUS 20:14

Meats for the belly, and the belly for meats: but God shall destroy both it and them. Now the body is not for fornication, but for the Lord; and the Lord for the body.

And God hath both raised up the Lord, and will also raise up us by his own power.

Know ye not that your bodies are the members of Christ? shall I then take the members of Christ, and make them the members of an harlot? God forbid.

What? know ye not that he which is joined to an harlot is one body? for two, saith he, shall be one flesh.

But he that is joined unto the Lord is one spirit.

Flee fornication. Every sin that a man doeth is without the body; but he that committeth fornication sinneth against his own body.

What? know ye not that your body is the temple of the Holy Ghost which is in you, which ye have of God, and ye are not your own?

For ye are bought with a price: therefore glorify God in your body, and in your spirit, which are God's.

                                        1 CORINTHIANS 6:13–20

But fornication, and all uncleanness, or covetousness, let it not be once named among you, as becometh saints.

EPHESIANS 5:3

Lord Jesus,

my thoughts and actions are impure at times.
Please renew my mind.
Thank You for promising to forgive me
and consider me as white as snow. Amen.

Repentance

We long for revival,
but revival begins with
repentance.

NATALIE GRANT

The Lord is not slack concerning his promise, as some men count slackness; but is longsuffering to us-ward, not willing that any should perish, but that all should come to repentance.

2 PETER 3:9

And the times of this ignorance God winked at; but now commandeth all men every where to repent.   ACTS 17:30

He that covereth his sins
shall not prosper:
but whoso confesseth
and forsaketh them
shall have mercy.

PROVERBS 28:13

I will have mercy, and not sacrifice: for I am not come to call the righteous, but sinners to repentance.   MATTHEW 9:13

Likewise, I say unto you, there is joy in the presence of the angels of God over one sinner that repenteth.   LUKE 15:10

Remember therefore how thou hast received and heard, and hold fast, and repent. If therefore thou shalt not watch, I will come on thee as a thief, and thou shalt not know what hour I will come upon thee.   REVELATION 3:3

Or despisest thou the riches of his goodness and forbearance and longsuffering; not knowing that the goodness of God leadeth thee to repentance?   ROMANS 2:4

Seek ye the LORD while he may be found, call ye upon him while he is near:

Let the wicked forsake his way, and the unrighteous man his thoughts: and let him return unto the LORD, and he will have mercy upon him; and to our God, for he will abundantly pardon.   ISAIAH 55:6–7

He looketh upon men, and if any say, I have sinned, and perverted that which was right, and it profited me not;

He will deliver his soul from going into the pit, and his life shall see the light.   JOB 33:27–28

Turn unto the LORD your God: for he is gracious and merciful, slow to anger, and of great kindness, and repenteth him of the evil.   JOEL 2:13

Draw nigh to God, and he will draw nigh to you. Cleanse your hands, ye sinners; and purify your hearts, ye double minded.   JAMES 4:8

Repent ye therefore, and be converted, that your sins may be blotted out, when the times of refreshing shall come from the presence of the Lord.   ACTS 3:19

Repent therefore of this thy wickedness, and pray God, if perhaps the thought of thine heart may be forgiven thee.   ACTS 8:22

The time is fulfilled, and the kingdom of God is at hand: repent ye, and believe the gospel.   MARK 1:15

The LORD is nigh unto them that are of a broken heart; and saveth such as be of a contrite spirit.   PSALM 34:18

Father,

I come to You to repent of my sins.
Change my heart and my desires, Lord,
so that from this day on I leave my sins in the past.
Amen.

Rest

gain and again,
I've found Him faithful to respond,
and the closer I move to Him,
the safer I feel and the better I rest.

PATSY CLAIRMONT

Six days may work be done; but in the seventh is the sabbath
of rest, holy to the LORD.   EXODUS 31:15

It is vain for you to rise up early, to sit up late, to eat the bread
of sorrows: for so he giveth his beloved sleep.   PSALM 127:2

When thou liest down,
thou shalt not be afraid:
yea, thou shalt lie down,
and thy sleep shall be sweet.

PROVERBS 3:24

I will both lay me down in peace, and sleep: for thou, LORD,
only makest me dwell in safety.   PSALM 4:8

For he spake in a certain place of the seventh day on this wise,
And God did rest the seventh day from all his works.
    There remaineth therefore a rest to the people of God.
                                          HEBREWS 4:4, 9

Rest in the LORD, and wait patiently for him: fret not thyself
because of him who prospereth in his way, because of the man
who bringeth wicked devices to pass.   PSALM 37:7

And thou shalt be secure, because there is hope; yea, thou shalt dig about thee, and thou shalt take thy rest in safety.

JOB 11:18

He that dwelleth in the secret place of the most High shall abide under the shadow of the Almighty.   PSALM 91:1

Slow me down, Lord.
My schedule gets so hectic that I find myself
with my priorities in the wrong order.
Grant me a few moments of quiet,
so that I may collect my thoughts and be refreshed.
Amen.

Righteousness

We do not have to be
qualified to be holy.

MADELEINE L'ENGLE

Blessed are they which do hunger and thirst after righteousness: for they shall be filled.   MATTHEW 5:6

A righteous man hateth lying: but a wicked man is loathsome, and cometh to shame.   PROVERBS 13:5

Know ye not that the unrighteous shall not inherit the kingdom of God? Be not deceived.   1 CORINTHIANS 6:9

But seek ye first the kingdom of God, and his righteousness; and all these things shall be added unto you.   MATTHEW 6:33

LORD, who shall abide in thy tabernacle? who shall dwell in thy holy hill?
    He that walketh uprightly, and worketh righteousness, and speaketh the truth in his heart.   PSALM 15:1–2

He withdraweth not his eyes from the righteous: but with kings are they on the throne; yea, he doth establish them for ever, and they are exalted.   JOB 36:7

Thy word is true from the beginning: and every one of thy righteous judgments endureth for ever.   PSALM 119:160

Then shall the righteous shine forth as the sun in the kingdom of their Father. Who hath ears to hear, let him hear.
                    MATTHEW 13:43

But if thou shalt indeed obey his voice, and do all that I speak; then I will be an enemy unto thine enemies, and an adversary unto thine adversaries.   EXODUS 23:22

The righteous cry, and the LORD heareth, and delivereth them out of all their troubles.   PSALM 34:17

Whereby are given unto us exceeding great and precious promises: that by these ye might be partakers of the divine nature, having escaped the corruption that is in the world through lust.
                                                          2 PETER 1:4

The eyes of the LORD
are upon the righteous,
and his ears are open
unto their cry.

PSALM 34:15

If we confess our sins, he is faithful and just to forgive us our sins, and to cleanse us from all unrighteousness.   1 JOHN 1:9

Ye that love the LORD, hate evil: he preserveth the souls of his saints; he delivereth them out of the hand of the wicked.
       Light is sown for the righteous.   PSALM 97:10–11

Then shall thy light break forth as the morning, and thine health shall spring forth speedily: and thy righteousness shall go before thee; the glory of the LORD shall be thy rearward.
                                                          ISAIAH 58:8

And it shall come to pass, if thou shalt hearken diligently unto the voice of the LORD thy God, to observe and to do all his commandments which I command thee this day, that the LORD thy God will set thee on high above all nations of the earth.

DEUTERONOMY 28:1

The LORD will not suffer the soul of the righteous to famish: but he casteth away the substance of the wicked.

PROVERBS 10:3

Blessed are they which are persecuted for righteousness' sake: for theirs is the kingdom of heaven.   MATTHEW 5:10

He that followeth after righteousness and mercy findeth life, righteousness, and honour.   PROVERBS 21:21

But know that the LORD hath set apart him that is godly for himself: the LORD will hear when I call unto him. PSALM 4:3

Then shall he answer them, saying, Verily I say unto you, Inasmuch as ye did it not to one of the least of these, ye did it not to me.

And these shall go away into everlasting punishment: but the righteous into life eternal.   MATTHEW 25:45–46

The righteous shall be glad in the LORD, and shall trust in him; and all the upright in heart shall glory.   PSALM 64:10

Dear God,

I want to seek after Your righteousness,
following what is eternal and true.
Thank You for Your faithfulness
in the times that I seek to do right,
even when I must stand alone.
Amen.

Salvation

Christ has made
all things right.
I had nothing to do
but accept it as
a free gift from Him.

HANNAH WHITALL SMITH

Therefore if any man be in Christ, he is a new creature: old things are passed away; behold, all things are become new.

2 CORINTHIANS 5:17

My little children, these things write I unto you, that ye sin not. And if any man sin, we have an advocate with the Father, Jesus Christ the righteous:

And he is the propitiation for our sins: and not for ours only, but also for the sins of the whole world.   1 JOHN 2:1–2

He that believeth on the Son
hath everlasting life.

JOHN 3:36

For this is good and acceptable in the sight of God our Saviour;

Who will have all men to be saved, and to come unto the knowledge of the truth.   1 TIMOTHY 2:3–4

But as many as received him, to them gave he power to become the sons of God, even to them that believe on his name.

Which were born, not of blood, nor of the will of the flesh, nor of the will of man, but of God.   JOHN 1:12–13

Neither is there salvation in any other: for there is none other name under heaven given among men, whereby we must be saved.   ACTS 4:12

But after that the kindness and love of God our Saviour toward man appeared,

Not by works of righteousness which we have done, but according to his mercy he saved us, by the washing of regeneration, and renewing of the Holy Ghost;

Which he shed on us abundantly through Jesus Christ our Saviour.   TITUS 3:4–6

For he hath made him to be sin for us, who knew no sin; that we might be made the righteousness of God in him.

2 CORINTHIANS 5:21

Even as I please all men in all things, not seeking mine own profit, but the profit of many, that they may be saved.

1 CORINTHIANS 10:33

Jesus answered and said unto him, Verily, verily, I say unto thee, Except a man be born again, he cannot see the kingdom of God.

Nicodemus saith unto him, How can a man be born when he is old? can he enter the second time into his mother's womb, and be born?

Jesus answered, Verily, verily, I say unto thee, Except a man be born of water and of the Spirit, he cannot enter into the kingdom of God.

That which is born of the flesh is flesh; and that which is born of the Spirit is spirit.

Marvel not that I said unto thee, Ye must be born again.

JOHN 3:3–7

Lord,

what a sacrifice You made in sending
Your only Son to die for me!
It should have been me sentenced to that horrible death,
but You saved me from the punishment that I deserve.
Thank You for the free gift of salvation.
Amen.

SCRIPTURE

How much of a calm and
gentle spirit you achieve, then,
will depend on how
regularly and consistently,
persistently and obediently you partake of
the Word of God,
your spiritual food.

SHIRLEY RICE

Let the word of Christ dwell in you richly in all wisdom; teaching and admonishing one another in psalms and hymns and spiritual songs, singing with grace in your hearts to the Lord.

COLOSSIANS 3:16

Thy word have I hid in mine heart, that I might not sin against thee.   PSALM 119:11

Thy word is a lamp
unto my feet,
and a light unto my path.

PSALM 119:105

For the word of God is quick, and powerful, and sharper than any twoedged sword, piercing even to the dividing asunder of soul and spirit, and of the joints and marrow, and is a discerner of the thoughts and intents of the heart.   HEBREWS 4:12

Therefore shall ye lay up these my words in your heart and in your soul, and bind them for a sign upon your hand, that they may be as frontlets between your eyes.

And ye shall teach them your children, speaking of them when thou sittest in thine house, and when thou walkest by the way, when thou liest down, and when thou risest up.

DEUTERONOMY 11:18–19

And that from a child thou hast known the holy scriptures, which are able to make thee wise unto salvation through faith which is in Christ Jesus.   2 TIMOTHY 3:15

So shall my word be that goeth forth out of my mouth: it shall not return unto me void, but it shall accomplish that which I please, and it shall prosper in the thing whereto I sent it.
                    ISAIAH 55:11

God, who at sundry times and in divers manners spake in time past unto the fathers by the prophets,

    Hath in these last days spoken unto us by his Son, whom he hath appointed heir of all things, by whom also he made the worlds.   HEBREWS 1:1–2

This book of the law shall not depart out of thy mouth; but thou shalt meditate therein day and night, that thou mayest observe to do according to all that is written therein: for then thou shalt make thy way prosperous, and then thou shalt have good success.   JOSHUA 1:8

Searching what, or what manner of time the Spirit of Christ which was in them did signify, when it testified beforehand the sufferings of Christ, and the glory that should follow.

    Unto whom it was revealed, that not unto themselves, but unto us they did minister the things, which are now reported unto you by them that have preached the gospel unto you with the Holy Ghost sent down from heaven; which things the angels desire to look into.   1 PETER 1:11–12

That ye may be mindful of the words which were spoken before by the holy prophets, and of the commandment of us the apostles of the Lord and Saviour.   2 PETER 3:2

Heavenly Father,

I want to hide Your Word in my heart.
Give me a clear mind as I
meditate on Scripture and memorize verses.
I want to have Your Truth in the forefront of my mind,
so that when I am faced with temptation or adversity,
I can refute it with Scripture as You did.
Thank You for the joy that fills my heart
as I reflect on Your Word. Amen.

Seeking God

For it is impossible to be
in the presence of Jesus
and not be changed.

JOANNA WEAVER

But seek ye first the kingdom of God, and his righteousness; and all these things shall be added unto you. MATTHEW 6:33

Sow to yourselves in righteousness, reap in mercy; break up your fallow ground: for it is time to seek the LORD, till he come and rain righteousness upon you. HOSEA 10:12

Seek the LORD and his strength, seek his face continually.
1 CHRONICLES 16:11

They that seek the Lord shall not want any good thing.

PSALM 34:10

Glory ye in his holy name: let the heart of them rejoice that seek the LORD. 1 CHRONICLES 16:10

But if from thence thou shalt seek the LORD thy God, thou shalt find him, if thou seek him with all thy heart and with all thy soul. DEUTERONOMY 4:29

One thing have I desired of the LORD, that will I seek after; that I may dwell in the house of the LORD all the days of my life, to behold the beauty of the LORD, and to enquire in his temple.
PSALM 27:4

And ye shall seek me, and find me, when ye shall search for me with all your heart.   JEREMIAH 29:13

With my soul have I desired thee in the night; yea, with my spirit within me will I seek thee early: for when thy judgments are in the earth, the inhabitants of the world will learn righteousness.   ISAIAH 26:9

And I say unto you, Ask, and it shall be given you; seek, and ye shall find; knock, and it shall be opened unto you. LUKE 11:9

Therefore came I forth to meet thee, diligently to seek thy face, and I have found thee.   PROVERBS 7:15

Seek the LORD, and ye shall live.   AMOS 5:6

If ye then be risen with Christ, seek those things which are above, where Christ sitteth on the right hand of God.
                                                  COLOSSIANS 3:1

Glory ye in his holy name: let the heart of them rejoice that seek the LORD.   1 CHRONICLES 16:10

If my people, which are called by my name, shall humble themselves, and pray, and seek my face, and turn from their wicked ways; then will I hear from heaven, and will forgive their sin, and will heal their land.   2 CHRONICLES 7:14

But rather seek ye the kingdom of God; and all these things shall be added unto you.   LUKE 12:31

Lord Jesus,

I want to have a growing, vital relationship with You.
Please don't let me fall into the complacency of
having a stagnant relationship with You.
I will only deepen my relationships with You
and with others when I invest my time.
Thank You for allowing me to
come into Your presence and meditate on You.
Amen.

Self-Control

Rules for proper behavior
keep us from getting hurt.
We risk our own life
and the lives of others when
we give in to our desires,
whatever they might be.

LINDA BARTLETT

Then said Pilate unto him, Hearest thou not how many things they witness against thee?

And he answered him to never a word; insomuch that the governor marvelled greatly.   MATTHEW 27:13–14

Yet Michael the archangel, when contending with the devil he disputed about the body of Moses, durst not bring against him a railing accusation, but said, The Lord rebuke thee.   JUDE 9

Let your moderation be
known unto all men.
The Lord is at hand.

PHILIPPIANS 4:5

For even hereunto were ye called: because Christ also suffered for us, leaving us an example, that ye should follow his steps:

Who did no sin, neither was guile found in his mouth:

Who, when he was reviled, reviled not again; when he suffered, he threatened not; but committed himself to him that judgeth righteously.   1 PETER 2:21–23

Charity suffereth long, and is kind; charity envieth not; charity vaunteth not itself, is not puffed up,

Doth not behave itself unseemly, seeketh not her own, is not easily provoked, thinketh no evil.   1 CORINTHIANS 13:4–5

Hast thou found honey? eat so much as is sufficient for thee, lest thou be filled therewith, and vomit it.   PROVERBS 25:16

Therefore let us not sleep, as do others; but let us watch and be sober.

For they that sleep sleep in the night; and they that be drunken are drunken in the night.   1 THESSALONIANS 5:6–7

If the spirit of the ruler rise up against thee, leave not thy place; for yielding pacifieth great offences.   ECCLESIASTES 10:4

Let us walk honestly, as in the day; not in rioting and drunkenness, not in chambering and wantonness, not in strife and envying.

But put ye on the Lord Jesus Christ, and make not provision for the flesh, to fulfil the lusts thereof.

ROMANS 13:13–14

And beside this, giving all diligence, add to your faith virtue; and to virtue knowledge;

And to knowledge temperance; and to temperance patience; and to patience godliness.   2 PETER 1:5–6

And every man that striveth for the mastery is temperate in all things. Now they do it to obtain a corruptible crown; but we an incorruptible.   1 CORINTHIANS 9:25

He sitteth alone and keepeth silence, because he hath borne it upon him.

He putteth his mouth in the dust; if so be there may be hope.   LAMENTATIONS 3:28–29

Teaching us that, denying ungodliness and worldly lusts, we should live soberly, righteously, and godly, in this present world.   TITUS 2:12

Be sober, grave,
temperate, sound in faith,
in charity, in patience.

TITUS 2:2

But I keep under my body, and bring it into subjection: lest that by any means, when I have preached to others, I myself should be a castaway.   1 CORINTHIANS 9:27

Neither fornicators, nor idolaters, nor adulterers, nor effeminate, nor abusers of themselves with mankind,
    Nor thieves, nor covetous, nor drunkards, nor revilers, nor extortioners, shall inherit the kingdom of God.
    And such were some of you: but ye are washed, but ye are sanctified, but ye are justified in the name of the Lord Jesus, and by the Spirit of our God.   1 CORINTHIANS 6:9–11

For if ye live after the flesh, ye shall die: but if ye through the Spirit do mortify the deeds of the body, ye shall live.
                                                   ROMANS 8:13

Be grave, not doubletongued, not given to much wine, not greedy of filthy lucre.   1 TIMOTHY 3:8

Dear God,

*I need You to help me resist going along with the crowd
when they do things that would displease You.
Let my words and actions be a constant beacon,
drawing the lost to You. Amen.*

Sin

It is the very nature of sin
to prevent man
from meditating
on spiritual things.

Mary Martha Sherwood

Therefore if any man be in Christ, he is a new creature: old things are passed away; behold, all things are become new.
2 CORINTHIANS 5:17

For I will be merciful to their unrighteousness, and their sins and their iniquities will I remember no more. HEBREWS 8:12

But if we walk in the light, as he is in the light, we have fellowship one with another, and the blood of Jesus Christ his Son cleanseth us from all sin.   1 JOHN 1:7

Come now, and let us reason together, saith the LORD: though your sins be as scarlet, they shall be as white as snow; though they be red like crimson, they shall be as wool.   ISAIAH 1:18

But he was wounded for our transgressions, he was bruised for our iniquities: the chastisement of our peace was upon him; and with his stripes we are healed.

All we like sheep have gone astray; we have turned every one to his own way; and the LORD hath laid on him the iniquity of us all.   ISAIAH 53:5–6

My little children, these things write I unto you, that ye sin not. And if any man sin, we have an advocate with the Father, Jesus Christ the righteous:

And he is the propitiation for our sins: and not for ours only, but also for the sins of the whole world.   1 JOHN 2:1–2

To him give all the prophets witness, that through his name whosoever believeth in him shall receive remission of sins.
ACTS 10:43

Knowing this, that our old man is crucified with him, that the body of sin might be destroyed, that henceforth we should not serve sin.

For he that is dead is freed from sin.   ROMANS 6:6–7

For this is my blood of the new testament, which is shed for many for the remission of sins.   MATTHEW 26:28

As far as the east is from the west,
so far hath he removed
our transgressions from us.

PSALM 103:12

This is a faithful saying, and worthy of all acceptation, that Christ Jesus came into the world to save sinners; of whom I am chief.   1 TIMOTHY 1:15

Who his own self bare our sins in his own body on the tree, that we, being dead to sins, should live unto righteousness: by whose stripes ye were healed.   1 PETER 2:24

Who gave himself for our sins, that he might deliver us from this present evil world, according to the will of God and our Father.   GALATIANS 1:4

Lord Jesus,

I ask forgiveness for the sins that I've committed, even today.
I repent of them now,
asking You to help me leave them in the past.
Nothing is worth separating me from You.
I pray that You will give me the strength to defeat Satan
and his attempts to keep me from living a life of victory. Amen.

Sincerity

Speaking beautifully is
little to the purpose
unless one lives
beautifully.

ELIZABETH PRENTISS

Blessed is the man unto whom the LORD imputeth not iniquity, and in whose spirit there is no guile.   PSALM 32:2

And in their mouth was found no guile: for they are without fault before the throne of God.   REVELATION 14:5

Wherefore gird up the loins of your mind, be sober, and hope to the end for the grace that is to be brought unto you at the revelation of Jesus Christ.   1 PETER 1:13

But let us, who are of the day, be sober, putting on the breastplate of faith and love; and for an helmet, the hope of salvation.
                          1 THESSALONIANS 5:8

As newborn babes, desire the sincere milk of the word, that ye may grow thereby.   1 PETER 2:2

For we are not as many, which corrupt the word of God: but as of sincerity, but as of God, in the sight of God speak we in Christ.   2 CORINTHIANS 2:17

Now therefore fear the LORD, and serve him in sincerity and in truth.   JOSHUA 24:14

Now the end of the commandment is charity out of a pure heart, and of a good conscience, and of faith unfeigned.
                          1 TIMOTHY 1:5

Therefore let us keep the feast, not with old leaven, neither with the leaven of malice and wickedness; but with the unleavened bread of sincerity and truth.   1 CORINTHIANS 5:8

Let love be without dissimulation. Abhor that which is evil; cleave to that which is good.   ROMANS 12:9

Seeing ye have purified your souls in obeying the truth through the Spirit unto unfeigned love of the brethren, see that ye love one another with a pure heart fervently.   1 PETER 1:22

What will ye do in the solemn day, and in the day of the feast of the LORD?   HOSEA 9:5

Grace be with all them that
love our Lord Jesus Christ
in sincerity. Amen.

EPHESIANS 6:24

I speak not by commandment, but by occasion of the forwardness of others, and to prove the sincerity of your love.
    2 CORINTHIANS 8:8

Wherefore laying aside all malice, and all guile, and hypocrisies, and envies, and all evil speakings.   1 PETER 2:1

That ye may approve things that are excellent; that ye may be sincere and without offence till the day of Christ.
    PHILIPPIANS 1:10

For our exhortation was not of deceit, nor of uncleanness, nor in guile:

But as we were allowed of God to be put in trust with the gospel, even so we speak; not as pleasing men, but God, which trieth our hearts.

For neither at any time used we flattering words, as ye know, nor a cloke of covetousness; God is witness.

1 THESSALONIANS 2:3–5

For I say, through the grace given unto me, to every man that is among you, not to think of himself more highly than he ought to think; but to think soberly, according as God hath dealt to every man the measure of faith.   ROMANS 12:3

For our rejoicing is this, the testimony of our conscience, that in simplicity and godly sincerity, not with fleshly wisdom, but by the grace of God, we have had our conversation in the world, and more abundantly to you-ward.   2 CORINTHIANS 1:12

Lord,

I pray that I will be sincere in my speech and actions.
Please help me refrain from using flattering words dishonestly.
Let me be genuine so that others can see You in me.
Amen.

Sobriety

"Abstain," says God.
He doesn't say, "Be careful"
or "Pray about it."
He says, "Abstain! Run from it! Don't touch it!
Have nothing to do with it!"
Stay pure and blameless.
If you don't,
God will suffer most of all.

ANNE ORTLUND

Drunkenness, revellings, and such like: of the which I tell you before, as I have also told you in time past, that they which do such things shall not inherit the kingdom of God.

GALATIANS 5:21

Whoredom and wine and new wine take away the heart.

HOSEA 4:11

For he shall be great in the sight of the Lord, and shall drink neither wine nor strong drink; and he shall be filled with the Holy Ghost, even from his mother's womb.   LUKE 1:15

For the drunkard and the glutton shall come to poverty: and drowsiness shall clothe a man with rags.   PROVERBS 23:21

And they have cast lots for my people; and have given a boy for an harlot, and sold a girl for wine, that they might drink.

JOEL 3:3

Who hath woe? who hath sorrow? who hath contentions? who hath babbling? who hath wounds without cause? who hath redness of eyes?

They that tarry long at the wine; they that go to seek mixed wine.

Look not thou upon the wine when it is red, when it giveth his colour in the cup, when it moveth itself aright.

At the last it biteth like a serpent, and stingeth like an adder.

PROVERBS 23:29–32

Now therefore beware, I pray thee, and drink not wine nor strong drink, and eat not any unclean thing.   JUDGES 13:4

Woe unto them that rise up early in the morning, that they may follow strong drink; that continue until night, till wine inflame them!   ISAIAH 5:11

Wine is a mocker,
strong drink is raging:
and whosoever is deceived thereby is not wise.

PROVERBS 20:1

Woe unto him that giveth his neighbour drink, that puttest thy bottle to him, and makest him drunken also, that thou mayest look on their nakedness!   HABAKKUK 2:15

And take heed to yourselves, lest at any time your hearts be overcharged with surfeiting, and drunkenness, and cares of this life, and so that day come upon you unawares.   LUKE 21:34

For while they be folden together as thorns, and while they are drunken as drunkards, they shall be devoured as stubble fully dry.   NAHUM 1:10

Dear God,

I dedicate my mind to You.
May I keep it clear and focused on You.
Give me the strength to say "no" to temptation.
Thank You for the free will that You have given to me—
I choose You and Your way.
Amen.

Strength

We must continue to
ask God for wisdom
and insight and for the strength to persevere.
He will cause us to rise up
and fly like eagles,
walking and not fainting.

NORMA SMALLEY

For the eyes of the LORD run to and fro throughout the whole earth, to shew himself strong in the behalf of them whose heart is perfect toward him.   2 CHRONICLES 16:9

Both riches and honour come of thee, and thou reignest over all; and in thine hand is power and might; and in thine hand it is to make great, and to give strength unto all.

1 CHRONICLES 29:12

Finally, my brethren, be strong in the Lord, and in the power of his might.   EPHESIANS 6:10

By pureness, by knowledge, by longsuffering, by kindness, by the Holy Ghost, by love unfeigned,

By the word of truth, by the power of God, by the armour of righteousness on the right hand and on the left.

2 CORINTHIANS 6:6–7

He giveth power to the faint; and to them that have no might he increaseth strength.   ISAIAH 40:29

Wait on the LORD: be of good courage, and he shall strengthen thine heart: wait, I say, on the LORD.   PSALM 27:14

But they that wait upon the LORD shall renew their strength; they shall mount up with wings as eagles; they shall run, and not be weary; and they shall walk, and not faint.

ISAIAH 40:31

The LORD will give strength unto his people; the LORD will bless his people with peace.   PSALM 29:11

My flesh and my heart faileth: but God is the strength of my heart, and my portion for ever.   PSALM 73:26

I know both how to be abased, and I know how to abound: every where and in all things I am instructed both to be full and to be hungry, both to abound and to suffer need.

I can do all things through Christ which strengtheneth me.
PHILIPPIANS 4:12–13

*T*he righteous also shall hold on his way,
and he that hath clean hands
shall be stronger and stronger.

JOB 17:9

That ye might walk worthy of the Lord unto all pleasing, being fruitful in every good work, and increasing in the knowledge of God;

Strengthened with all might, according to his glorious power, unto all patience and longsuffering with joyfulness.
COLOSSIANS 1:10–11

And he said unto me, My grace is sufficient for thee: for my strength is made perfect in weakness. Most gladly therefore will I rather glory in my infirmities, that the power of Christ may rest upon me.   2 CORINTHIANS 12:9

O God, thou art terrible out of thy holy places: the God of
Israel is he that giveth strength and power unto his people.
Blessed be God.   PSALM 68:35

The LORD is my rock, and my fortress, and my deliverer; my
God, my strength, in whom I will trust; my buckler, and the
horn of my salvation, and my high tower.   PSALM 18:2

Father,
help me to see today how I can be useful.
Then give me the strength to walk into
the opportunities You have set before me.
Amen.

Temptation

Temptations come,
as a general rule,
when they are sought.

MARGARET OLIPHANT

Blessed is the man that endureth temptation: for when he is tried, he shall receive the crown of life, which the Lord hath promised to them that love him.   JAMES 1:12

Because thou hast kept the word of my patience, I also will keep thee from the hour of temptation, which shall come upon all the world, to try them that dwell upon the earth.
REVELATION 3:10

Let no man say when he is tempted, I am tempted of God: for God cannot be tempted with evil, neither tempteth he any man.
JAMES 1:13

And lead us not into temptation, but deliver us from evil: For thine is the kingdom, and the power, and the glory, for ever. Amen.   MATTHEW 6:13

The Lord knoweth how to deliver the godly out of temptations.
2 PETER 2:9

Watch and pray, that ye enter not into temptation: the spirit indeed is willing, but the flesh is weak.   MATTHEW 26:41

And when he was at the place, he said unto them, Pray that ye enter not into temptation.   LUKE 22:40

There hath no temptation taken you but such as is common to man: but God is faithful, who will not suffer you to be tempted above that ye are able; but will with the temptation also make a way to escape, that ye may be able to bear it.
1 CORINTHIANS 10:13

Thank You, Lord,

that You understand.
Keep reminding me that You were in all ways
tempted just like I am, yet without sin.
It's so comforting to know that You have
walked this same path and were victorious.
Amen.

Truth

If we are Christians,
we have committed ourselves to
the Lord Jesus Christ
who said, "I am the Truth."
In giving ourselves to Him,
we dedicate ourselves
to the truth
not only about Him
but about ourselves.

PAMELA HOOVER HEIM

God is a Spirit: and they that worship him must worship him in spirit and in truth.   JOHN 4:24

Even the Spirit of truth; whom the world cannot receive, because it seeth him not, neither knoweth him: but ye know him; for he dwelleth with you, and shall be in you.   JOHN 14:17

That he who blesseth himself in the earth shall bless himself in the God of truth; and he that sweareth in the earth shall swear by the God of truth.   ISAIAH 65:16

And ye shall know the truth,
and the truth shall
make you free.

JOHN 8:32

He is the Rock, his work is perfect: for all his ways are judgment: a God of truth and without iniquity, just and right is he.
                                            DEUTERONOMY 32:4

Finally, brethren, whatsoever things are true, whatsoever things are honest, whatsoever things are just, whatsoever things are pure, whatsoever things are lovely, whatsoever things are of good report; if there be any virtue, and if there be any praise, think on these things.   PHILIPPIANS 4:8

Buy the truth, and sell it not; also wisdom, and instruction, and understanding.   PROVERBS 23:23

For the LORD is good; his mercy is everlasting; and his truth endureth to all generations.   PSALM 100:5

Jesus saith unto him, I am the way, the truth, and the life: no man cometh unto the Father, but by me.   JOHN 14:6

For the word of the LORD is right; and all his works are done in truth.   PSALM 33:4

And for their sakes I sanctify myself, that they also might be sanctified through the truth.   JOHN 17:19

These are the things that ye shall do; Speak ye every man the truth to his neighbour; execute the judgment of truth and peace in your gates.   ZECHARIAH 8:16

For the law was given by Moses, but grace and truth came by Jesus Christ.   JOHN 1:17

Father,

You are the Source of Truth.
Teach me what is true concerning You,
and give me the courage to seek the truth about myself.
I am thankful that truth will triumph,
and that the followers of truth will be victorious.
Amen.

Understanding

Yearn to understand first
and to be understood second.

BECA LEWIS ALLEN

Happy is the man that findeth wisdom, and the man that getteth understanding.

For the merchandise of it is better than the merchandise of silver, and the gain thereof than fine gold.

She is more precious than rubies: and all the things thou canst desire are not to be compared unto her.

PROVERBS 3:13–15

Then shalt thou understand the fear of the LORD, and find the knowledge of God.

For the LORD giveth wisdom: out of his mouth cometh knowledge and understanding.   PROVERBS 2:5–6

They shall not hurt nor destroy in all my holy mountain: for the earth shall be full of the knowledge of the LORD, as the waters cover the sea.

And in that day there shall be a root of Jesse, which shall stand for an ensign of the people; to it shall the Gentiles seek: and his rest shall be glorious.   ISAIAH 11:9–10

When wisdom entereth into thine heart, and knowledge is pleasant unto thy soul;

Discretion shall preserve thee, understanding shall keep thee:

To deliver thee from the way of the evil man.

PROVERBS 2:10–12

If there be therefore any consolation in Christ, if any comfort of love, if any fellowship of the Spirit, if any bowels and mercies,

Fulfil ye my joy, that ye be likeminded, having the same love, being of one accord, of one mind.   PHILIPPIANS 2:1–2

Justice and judgment are the habitation of thy throne: mercy and truth shall go before thy face.   PSALM 89:14

When I was a child, I spake as a child, I understood as a child, I thought as a child: but when I became a man, I put away childish things.   1 CORINTHIANS 13:11

The tongue of the wise
useth knowledge aright:
but the mouth of fools
poureth out foolishness.

PROVERBS 15:2

In the lips of him that hath understanding wisdom is found: but a rod is for the back of him that is void of understanding.   PROVERBS 10:13

But thou, O Lord, art a God full of compassion, and gracious, longsuffering, and plenteous in mercy and truth.   PSALM 86:15

But let him that glorieth glory in this, that he understandeth and knoweth me, that I am the LORD which exercise lovingkindness, judgment, and righteousness, in the earth: for in these things I delight, saith the LORD.   JEREMIAH 9:24

And unto man he said, Behold, the fear of the Lord, that is wisdom; and to depart from evil is understanding.   JOB 28:28

With the ancient is wisdom; and in length of days understanding.
    With him is wisdom and strength, he hath counsel and understanding.   JOB 12:12–13

Wisdom resteth in the heart of him that hath understanding: but that which is in the midst of fools is made known.
                                        PROVERBS 14:33

Evil men understand not judgment: but they that seek the LORD understand all things.   PROVERBS 28:5

But as it is written, Eye hath not seen, nor ear heard, neither have entered into the heart of man, the things which God hath prepared for them that love him.
    But God hath revealed them unto us by his Spirit: for the Spirit searcheth all things, yea, the deep things of God.
    For what man knoweth the things of a man, save the spirit of man which is in him? even so the things of God knoweth no man, but the Spirit of God.   1 CORINTHIANS 2:9–11

Folly is joy to him that is destitute of wisdom: but a man of understanding walketh uprightly.   PROVERBS 15:21

The heart of the prudent getteth knowledge; and the ear of the wise seeketh knowledge.   PROVERBS 18:15

Make me to understand the way of thy precepts: so shall I talk of thy wondrous works.   PSALM 119:27

For if these things be in you, and abound, they make you that ye shall neither be barren nor unfruitful in the knowledge of our Lord Jesus Christ.   2 PETER 1:8

The rich man is wise in his own conceit; but the poor that hath understanding searcheth him out.   PROVERBS 28:11

Teach me good judgment and knowledge: for I have believed thy commandments.   PSALM 119:66

The heart of him that hath understanding seeketh knowledge: but the mouth of fools feedeth on foolishness.

PROVERBS 15:14

For to one is given by the Spirit the word of wisdom; to another the word of knowledge by the same Spirit.

1 CORINTHIANS 12:8

Lord,
I often feel misunderstood.
But thank You for understanding me.
Help me to turn to You,
accepting Your will for my life.
When I can't understand Your plan,
help me to trust in You.
Amen.

Unity

The Word tells us that
He has called His children to be
one with Him and with each other.
In order for His will to be realized,
we must first unite.
To unite simply means to join.

KATHERYN BOONE

Can two walk together, except they be agreed?   AMOS 3:3

Behold, how good and how pleasant it is for brethren to dwell together in unity!   PSALM 133:1

Be of the same mind one toward another.   ROMANS 12:16

Now the God of patience and consolation grant you to be like-minded one toward another according to Christ Jesus:
    That ye may with one mind and one mouth glorify God, even the Father of our Lord Jesus Christ.   ROMANS 15:5–6

Let him seek peace, and ensue it.   1 PETER 3:11

Now I beseech you, brethren, by the name of our Lord Jesus Christ, that ye all speak the same thing, and that there be no divisions among you; but that ye be perfectly joined together in the same mind and in the same judgment.
          1 CORINTHIANS 1:10

Like snowflakes,

Lord, your children are so different.
Nationality, personality, appearance,
or talent make no difference with You.
Your love is the same for each individual.
May I treat everyone equally as You do.
Thank You that we're all special in Your sight.
Amen.

Wisdom

Learning is not attained
by chance,
it must be sought for
with ardor and attended to with diligence.

ABIGAIL ADAMS

A wise man's heart discerneth both time and judgment.

ECCLESIASTES 8:5

Be wise now therefore, O ye kings: be instructed, ye judges of the earth.   PSALM 2:10

Say unto wisdom, Thou art my sister; and call understanding thy kinswoman.   PROVERBS 7:4

A prudent man foreseeth the evil,
and hideth himself:
but the simple pass on,
and are punished.

PROVERBS 22:3

Wherefore be ye not unwise, but understanding what the will of the Lord is.   EPHESIANS 5:17

A good man sheweth favour, and lendeth: he will guide his affairs with discretion.   PSALM 112:5

He that handleth a matter wisely shall find good: and whoso trusteth in the LORD, happy is he.
    The wise in heart shall be called prudent: and the sweetness of the lips increaseth learning.   PROVERBS 16:20–21

The LORD by wisdom hath founded the earth; by understanding hath he established the heavens.

By his knowledge the depths are broken up, and the clouds drop down the dew.

My son, let not them depart from thine eyes: keep sound wisdom and discretion.   PROVERBS 3:19–21

Therefore whosoever heareth these sayings of mine, and doeth them, I will liken him unto a wise man, which built his house upon a rock:

And the rain descended, and the floods came, and the winds blew, and beat upon that house; and it fell not: for it was founded upon a rock.   MATTHEW 7:24–25

He that is void of wisdom despiseth his neighbour: but a man of understanding holdeth his peace.   PROVERBS 11:12

I wisdom dwell with prudence, and find out knowledge of witty inventions.   PROVERBS 8:12

A prudent man concealeth knowledge: but the heart of fools proclaimeth foolishness.   PROVERBS 12:23

Who is wise, and he shall understand these things? prudent, and he shall know them? for the ways of the LORD are right, and the just shall walk in them: but the transgressors shall fall therein.   HOSEA 14:9

How much better is it to get wisdom than gold! and to get understanding rather to be chosen than silver!
                    PROVERBS 16:16

My son, attend to my words; incline thine ear unto my sayings.

Let them not depart from thine eyes; keep them in the midst of thine heart.

For they are life unto those that find them, and health to all their flesh.　　PROVERBS 4:20–22

The law of the wise is a fountain of life, to depart from the snares of death.

Good understanding giveth favour: but the way of transgressors is hard.　　PROVERBS 13:14–15

With him is strength and wisdom: the deceived and the deceiver are his.

He leadeth counsellors away spoiled, and maketh the judges fools.　　JOB 12:16–17

My son, eat thou honey, because it is good; and the honeycomb, which is sweet to thy taste:

So shall the knowledge of wisdom be unto thy soul: when thou hast found it, then there shall be a reward, and thy expectation shall not be cut off.　　PROVERBS 24:13–14

Howbeit we speak wisdom among them that are perfect: yet not the wisdom of this world, nor of the princes of this world, that come to nought:

But we speak the wisdom of God in a mystery, even the hidden wisdom, which God ordained before the world unto our glory:

Which none of the princes of this world knew: for had they known it, they would not have crucified the Lord of glory.

1 CORINTHIANS 2:6–8

And wisdom and knowledge shall be the stability of thy times, and strength of salvation: the fear of the LORD is his treasure.

ISAIAH 33:6

Whoso is wise,
and will observe these things,
even they shall understand
the loving kindness of the Lord.

PSALM 107:43

For your obedience is come abroad unto all men. I am glad therefore on your behalf: but yet I would have you wise unto that which is good, and simple concerning evil.   ROMANS 16:19

And they that be wise shall shine as the brightness of the firmament; and they that turn many to righteousness as the stars for ever and ever.   DANIEL 12:3

If any of you lack wisdom, let him ask of God, that giveth to all men liberally, and upbraideth not; and it shall be given him.

JAMES 1:5

I will instruct thee and teach thee in the way which thou shalt go: I will guide thee with mine eye.   PSALM 32:8

The simple believeth every word: but the prudent man looketh well to his going.   PROVERBS 14:15

And if any man think that he knoweth any thing, he knoweth nothing yet as he ought to know.   1 CORINTHIANS 8:2

For wisdom is a defence, and money is a defence: but the excellency of knowledge is, that wisdom giveth life to them that have it.   ECCLESIASTES 7:12

Lord Jesus,
You have promised that if I ask for wisdom,
You will give it to me.
I ask for a sharp mind and sound judgment
to be used for Your glory.
Amen.